VIEWFINDERS

ALSO BY JEANNE MOUTOUSSAMY-ASHE

DAUFUSKIE ISLAND:
A Photographic Essay

Kali Diana Grosvenor

Research Assistant

—————◄◆◆►—————

Deborah Willis-Ryan

Consultant

VIEWFINDERS

Black Women Photographers

by Jeanne Moutoussamy-Ashe

D O D D ,   M E A D   &   C O M P A N Y

New York

No part of this book may be reproduced in any form
without permission in writing from the publisher.
Published by Dodd, Mead & Company, Inc.
79 Madison Avenue, New York, N.Y. 10016
Distributed in Canada by
McClelland and Stewart Limited, Toronto
Manufactured in the United States of America
Designed by Claire B. Counihan

First Edition

Library of Congress Cataloging in Publication Data

Moutoussamy-Ashe, Jeanne, 1951–
Viewfinders: black women photographers,

Bibliography: p.
Includes index.
1. Afro-American photographers—United States—
Biography. 2. Women photographers—United States—
Biography. I. Title.
TR139.M63 1985   770′.92′2 [B]   85-16233
ISBN 0-396-08609-8
ISBN 0-396-08611-X (pbk.)

*This book is dedicated
to black women photographers
past and present.*

Contents

―――――◄●●►―――――

Acknowledgments

I would like to thank several people for their time and assistance in making this book possible.

Thanks go to my agent, Ivy Stone, who believes in the preservation of history and took great interest in seeing this book through. Thanks go to my editor, Margaret Norton, for her valuable insights and to Fifi Oscard for her encouragement.

I would also like to thank the staff at the Schomburg Center for their assistance, Howard Beeth at the Houston Public Library, Ann Vanriette Mills at the Danville Public Library, Judith Chase at the Old Slave Mart Museum, Daniel T. Williams at Tuskegee Institute, Valencia Hollins Coar, Herbert Nipson and Basil Phillips at *Ebony* magazine, Paul Robeson, Jr., Edwina Harleston Whitlock, Roland Charles at the Black Gallery, Collis Davis, Jr., Wilhelmina Wynn, and Mrs. Lucille Moore.

Many thanks go to Mr. John H. Johnson, publisher of *Ebony* magazine, for his generosity and support in contributing information and photographs to the book. No research on black culture would be complete without the aid of *Ebony* magazine, as it holds a wealth of information about black America and has remained consistent throughout the years.

I am grateful to Kip Branch for his assistance and support and to Marie Brown whose expertise was of great help to the manuscript. And to my husband, Arthur, whom I greatly appreciate for his insights on creative writing. Thanks go to Deborah Willis-Ryan whose dedication to the history of photography we should all be eternally grateful for.

I could not have completed this book without the assistance of my researcher and friend, Kali Grosvenor, whose unlimited availability, hard work and enthusiasm made working on this project fun even during the difficult and trying stages of pulling together large amounts of information and numerous people. A special thank you to Derilene McCloud who worked many long hours on the book, keeping it and me organized throughout its entire production. Her enthusiasm and dedication to the subject was also an inspiration to the book.

And lastly, I would like to thank all of the black women photographers for their cooperation, time, and assistance in putting this book together. They have been more than patient in awaiting their due recognition. I hope they will be pleased with the book.

Jeanne Moutoussamy-Ashe

Introduction

Among nineteenth-century black women were poets, opera singers, inventors, sculptors, painters, and photographers. Under slavery, black women organized benevolent and burial societies. They were among the agents and conductors of the underground railroad. They founded colleges and orphanages and were active in the abolitionist movement. Black women saw to the needs of the black soldier during the Civil War, nursing him and often teaching him. There were the familiar names: Harriet Tubman, Sojourner Truth, and Ida Wells Barnett, the organizer of the antilynching movement. But there were also many lesser-known women, such as Lucy Terry, the first black female poet in America; the sculptor Edmonia Lewis, born of a free father and a Chippewa mother, who attended Oberlin College and went to Rome in 1865 to study art. There was Madame Sissieretta Jones, a nineteenth-century coloratura soprano who toured Europe and South America.[1]

Although there have been several attempts to establish black women's archives, only a few have been successfully maintained over the years. A significant body of material, collected during the 1940s, 1950s, and 1960s, forms the core of the Bethune Museum–Archives, which opened in 1979 in Mary McLeod Bethune's former home, located in Washington, D.C., now a national historic site.

There is growing interest in the contributions of black women to America's heritage. As this introduction is being written, Bethune is being honored with a commemorative stamp bearing her likeness; she is only the eighth black American—and the only black woman besides Harriet

Tubman—to be so honored. Unfortunately, the significant contributions of hundreds of black women have been lost to history—their works, papers, photographs—as the eleventh-hour attempt to fill in the gaps and document their roles begins. One of the most inspiring things in writing this book has been discovering not only the number of black women who have devoted themselves to photography but, more important, how these women dealt with forces that were much more oppressive and severe than those that women face today.

In part, the purpose of compiling a record of the black women who ventured into photography, both professionally and artistically, is to integrate the accomplishments and contributions they made with the history of photography, which to date has ignored their participation. As male-oriented a field as photography is, nonetheless quite a number of professional women have mastered its techniques; yet the few who have been mentioned historically have been white.

Although the problem of sexism exists, the problem of racism has presented more difficulties for black women photographers: they are confronted with both types of discrimination. There have been several occasions when I have personally been confronted by them. I have, on occasion, been hired by corporations such as IBM and AT&T, through advertising agencies, to fill their equal opportunity employment quotas. There is no question that corporate work pays photographers very well. Unfortunately, however, the call for minority photographers comes once a year at best, and when it does, the company tries to spread the work among many of the black photographers who are also looking for work. While one job for one black photographer may be of significance to the equal opportunity employment program, to the black photographer it is not.

The early days of photography tested every photographer's patience and tenacity. All photographers worked with cumbersome equipment, but they had the perseverance to learn and develop new and easier techniques.

The photographer of the nineteenth and early twentieth centuries was a rarity compared with the situation today, when just about every American household has at least one camera. One photo dealer in New York City estimates total camera sales of four hundred million a year, and this is not just to the professional market. Today, professional photographic equipment competes with equipment that allows almost everyone to take photographs. On the other hand, because of the ease of the technical performance of cameras today, photographers are freer to deal with the compositional decisions that make great photographs. It is important to realize that although photography is the hobby of a great many people, the professional photographer is concerned with the intellectual challenges and creative decision making in the picture-making process. So often, when viewing photographs today, we may hear the comment, "I could have taken that!" This is an easy assumption to make in today's world. Something that Picasso once said is a good response to that statement: "But could you have *thought* of that?" Swept away by the ease of taking pictures, our response to looking at photographs has lacked awareness of the intellectual process of the actual execution of the photograph.

There is nothing more mysterious than a well-defined fact. The camera, as no other artistic tool, can convey one as truthfully as possible. Whether we choose to accept that fact—the photograph—or not is an individual choice. Viewing photographs as they are, without our individual biases, is the most fruitful way of looking at photographs. Photography should force us to question ourselves and to question the environment in which we live.

My interest in writing a book on black women photographers started in the spring of 1982 when, on a visit to Yale University's Beinecke Rare Books Library, I was looking at photographs from the Carl Van Vechten Collection. It was in this collection that I first saw photographs of well-known black Americans that were stamped with the name E. G. Robeson. I was excited, surprised, and proud to find out that these photographs were taken by Mrs. Paul Robeson. When I returned to New York City, I telephoned Deborah Willis-Ryan, the photograph specialist at the Schomburg Center for Research in Black Culture, to ask her if she knew about Eslanda Robeson's photographic work. Although she did not, she told me that she too had been interested in researching black women photographers lost to history. Deborah was already in the process of compiling her recently published bio-bibliography of black photographers, and she had a few names of some pioneer black women. She also informed me that a black woman scholar from Chicago, Valencia Hollins Coar, had just finished assembling a photographic exhibition, with a catalogue, entitled *A Century of Black Photographers 1840–1960*. But although the project was beautifully done and a badly needed contribution to photographic history, there was little mention of black women—only a brief mention of a few in the back of the catalogue—and no evidence of the photographs taken by them.

Being a black woman, I was concerned that no women were included in this important addition to photography's history. I knew that the women had existed, that I myself was not a true pioneer. And so my curiosity about the possibilities of finding those black women who had pursued the craft of photography grew. Deborah Willis-Ryan's demanding schedule at the Schomburg left her with little time to pursue the project, so with her initial guidance, I began the search for these lost women photographers. Once I found a publisher for the project, I devoted my time to completing the research and conducting interviews with the women so that, within a year, before any more photographers or their works could be lost, the information would be documented and compiled in a book.

While it has been an interesting and rewarding task, it has also been frustrating. While some of the still-living pioneer women were helpful in piecing together their photographic careers, there were others who refused to cooperate. The photographers included in the following pages were selected because of their accomplishments in the field of photography. The criteria used in selecting "accomplished" photographers were not limited to their contribution to the field of photography, however. Rather, "accomplished" refers to their ability to document their community or personal lives. Their inclusion here illustrates their ambition and drive to produce work, often while confronting adversity.

Although there are many contemporary black women photographers working in the field, this project was primarily focused on the pioneers. It is a tribute to them. What is included about contemporary black women photographers gives us an idea of the range of work being done by women today.

Historical research on black women is a difficult task. But

more specifically, historical research on the black woman photographer seemed impossible, since there was so little material available. This book only scratches the surface of the contributions black women have made to black history, American history, and photographic history. Nonetheless, its addition to the archives that have finally begun to appear on black women preserves at least some of these contributors' work and the stories about how they, and we, came to be. There are certainly many more women who should have been included in this book, and it is my hope that they will come forward and deposit their knowledge and work into the growing archives of the history of America's black women.

VIEWFINDERS

Part 1

HISTORICAL OVERVIEW

1839–1910

1. 1860 advertisement

Shortly before the Frenchman Louis Jacques Mandé Daguerre announced the discovery of photography to the world on August 19, 1839, the most famous slave revolt aboard a slaveship took place on the Spanish vessel *Amistad.* It touched off another revolt: the brig *Creole,* laden with slaves, sailed from Richmond bound for New Orleans; there the slaves mutinied, took the vessel, and carried her into the British West Indies and freedom. These two events, the mutinies and the discovery of photography, had a profound effect on black and white America's view of itself.

Photography, itself growing, documented the growth of America.[2] While Europe had its 2000-year-old history of art and culture, white America in the new republic became fascinated with photography, which was only fifty years younger than the republic itself. While Europe may have seen photography as something of a stepchild, America, in its own infancy, embraced the new science.

For black America, the *Amistad* mutiny played a key role in touching off heated controversy between antislavery and proslavery factions, heightening a positive awareness of black America's image of itself as a part of the young republic. Both events caused dramatic changes in the early development of America.

The first black in photography was a man named Jules Lion (sometimes incorrectly spelled Lyons). He studied the daguerreotype in Paris and later brought his knowledge and work to New Orleans, where a newspaper commended his work in the field as early as 1843.[3] But according to later records and 1860[4] advertisements (See Illus. #1), Lion was forced to sell his photographic apparatus when his business declined, making it impossible for him to continue with his craft.[5] This was not an unusual thing to happen to a black person in America in that period. The 1860s were a most difficult time in black America's history, as poverty, illiteracy, war, and social dismemberment made the success of small black businesses, which depended on black patrons, virtually impossible. It was also not surprising that the first black in photography learned his craft in Europe, because for the majority of black people during slavery, education was unattainable.[6]

African art reveals the artistry of the black people. But skilled African artists, when brought to America under conditions of slavery, were denied the opportunity to practice their traditional tribal arts. Because the majority of black people who lived in America before 1863 were slaves, most Afro-American artists who had any knowledge of the predominant American art forms were self-taught free persons from the North. Because black artists faced the insurmountable barrier of prejudice, a number of them left the United States for Europe, for training and for an opportunity to sell their work.[7] For example, Edmonia Lewis, a well-known female sculptor who was born in Albany, New York, in the 1840s and who used photographs to sculpt from,[8] left the United States to continue her work in Europe. Henry Tanner, the great painter from Pennsylvania, found life for a black artist in America too difficult and in 1891 left for France, where he spent the remainder of his life. While he received wide acclaim in Europe, he got only meager recognition in America.

America's contribution to art was small until African art came to the attention of European critics; they claimed that this primitive art was as sophisticated and imaginative as the art of many other civilizations. America's desire to create an American art free from European influence finally led to the acceptance of African art and artists.[9]

Although blacks became photographers shortly after the invention of photography, white historians have not included any blacks as contributors to the history, as thinkers or as producers of the medium or art form. This, though, is not new. What makes this historical deletion so important are quotes such as this one from Martin Sandler's 1979 book, *The Story of American Photography:* "Slowly but surely, photography was becoming an American folk art, the most democratic art the world has ever known."[10] Surely the author wasn't talking about the same "democratic art" that was used by photographer J. T. Zealy in documenting slaves on a Columbia, South Carolina, plantation in 1850. This group of fifteen daguerreotypes, which were discovered in 1977, were considered to be "important early daguerreotypes. Perhaps the most spectacular 'find' to date at the Peabody Museum at Harvard University."[11] But those same historians neglected to note that these "important daguerreotypes" were commissioned by Swiss zoologist and Harvard University professor Louis Agassiz for a scientific study on the anatomical details of "the African race" to bolster his theory that blacks were a separate species, separately created. The South Carolina slaves' owner, B. F. Taylor, glad to have scientific backing for his own belief in black inferiority, obliged Agassiz with fifteen

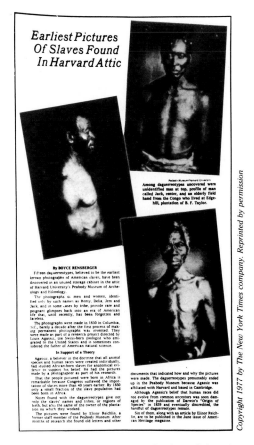

2. New York Times *article describing the earliest photos of slaves*

daguerreotypes of his slaves.[12] "Democratic art"?

The ambiguously "democratic art" was also exposed in this story of a woman slave in 1859.[13] Louisa Picquet was born a slave and was separated at the age of fourteen from her mother, Elizabeth Ramsey. The two managed to maintain communication through letters written by others, with the permission of their white slave masters. They frequently requested photographs from one another, for this was becoming a common way for people to keep mementos of each other, although it was not a common practice among slaves. In fact, it was a rarity and was only done with the money and permission of the slave owner. In one letter Mrs. Ramsey wrote:

March 8, 1859
Whorton, Texas

My Dear Daughter,
I want you to have your ambrotype taken also your children and send them to me I would give this world to see you and my sweet little children; my god bless you my dear child and protect you is my prayer.

Your Affectioned Mother
Elizabeth Ramsey

In a second letter, written after the daughter had answered her mother's letter and had also requested a daguerreotype, the slave mother answers her daughter's letter, writing,

It is not in our power to comply with your request in regard to the daguerreotypes this time, we shall move to Matagorde shortly, there I can comply with your request.

Elizabeth Ramsey

In a letter to Louisa, the owner of Elizabeth Ramsey wrote:

I send you by this mail a daguerreotype likeness of your mother and brother, which I hope you will receive. Your mother received yours in a damaged condition. . . .

Respec'y yours,
A. C. Horton

The daguerreotypes were described as "both taken on one plate, mother and son, and are set forth in their best possible gear, to impress us in the North with the superior condition of the slave over the free colored people,"[14] by the Reverend Mr. Mattison of the A.M.E. Church (circa 1860) in a letter he wrote for Louisa Picquet. In this case, photography was used by the slave owner as a way of making others think slaves were better off than free persons.

If indeed photography was a "democratic art," then it was so only to the extent that those who used the process were free to express themselves. If slaves were allowed to be creative, they were only to be creative in their menial labors, such as carpentry and basketry work for their slave owners.[15]

Meanwhile the 1850 U.S. census reported that there were 892 male daguerreotypists in the country, with the heaviest concentration in the Northeast. The state of New York reported 240, Pennsylvania 153.[16] Oddly enough, the state of Connecticut recorded only 53 daguerreotypists, but a separate 1850 census listing for free black males recorded a black daguerreotypist in one state—Connecticut.[17] This report did not include women in occupations. Women's occupations weren't listed in the U.S. census until 1870, and the census count at that time was not complete because of the confusion following the Civil War. As a result of the undercount, it was estimated that at least 500,000 Negroes and 750,000 whites were omitted from the 1870 census. The census did not begin to list black women's occupations until 1890, and even that census was undercounted.[18]

Although the 1850 census showed that slaves were primarily involved in agricultural work and secondarily in domestic and personal service, the exact numbers may never be known, since complete records of slaves and their many occupations were not preserved. Most black women were employed as maids, cooks, washerwomen, seamstresses, dressmakers, and midwives. However, blacks were engaged in practically all kinds of small business enterprise during the days of slavery. Most of these businesspeople lived in the North and were engaged in skilled trades and personal services.[19] Since in the South the slaves were kept ignorant and unlettered by slave owners, who prohibited their receiving any formal education, it was natural that most business ventures by Negroes were established in the North.[20]

As popular as the daguerreotype was, it lasted only about twelve years. At the beginning of the 1840s the average price for a daguerreotype, including its case, was two dollars. By the end of the 1840s, daguerreotypes were two for twenty-five cents. Competition drove prices down. But although the cost of daguerreotypes went down, few blacks used the process. The blacks who could afford to purchase a daguerreotype outfit were among the free blacks, and most free blacks were busy trying to defend and free the rest of the enslaved race. "Many of the Negroes who were leaders in whatever business was carried on up to about 1884 were the prominent workers in activities for race liberation and manhood privileges, thus subtracting energy and time from business pursuits.[21] Some slaves may have learned the photographic process in exchange for labor from a "liberal" slave owner. This owner would be "liberal" with respect to allowing his slave some access to education and learning. Occasionally, some enterprising black slave would purchase his freedom with the profits made from conducting some type of business enterprise. There were occasional instances of kindhearted white masters who permitted their slaves to peddle, or conduct small business enterprises in makeshift shops. With the money they earned, slaves were sometimes permitted to buy their own freedom. Some masters realized that it was advantageous to make the slaves more efficient by giving them necessary manual training, since economic life in the South at the time was mostly nonindustrial and manual skills played an

3. 1860 advertisement for sale of photography

important role in economic activity. In such instances, white businessmen taught their slaves not only how to develop skills to produce certain types of goods but also how to read and write and keep records. Later, this training would prove to be of great value to those who went into business on their own after their emancipation.[22]

Many new photographic processes were invented in the 1850s: The collodion or "wet plate" process, the carte de visite, the ambrotype, and the tintype. Around the same time, blacks began organizing to protest oppression and to advocate education so that they could leave menial occupations and aspire to mechanical, agricultural, and professional pursuits. Conventions to advocate opportunities and education for blacks were held in Columbus, Ohio, New York City, Rochester, and Philadelphia. There was a great need for schools and colleges for blacks. Frederick Douglass asserted that blacks had to learn new trades. More daguerreotype portrait studios began to appear all over the United States. There were more than ninety galleries in New York City alone. Although there has only been documentation of a few black male photographers in Pennsylvania and Michigan, it stands to reason that black women were also employed in some of the studios across the country, particularly in the North. Because photos were in such demand, shopkeepers, doctors, and craftsmen of all kinds opened these galleries as a sideline to their profession.

Any relationship black women had to photography before 1860 can only be documented through records kept by the established white photographers and free blacks who conducted photography as a business. Because of the confusion surrounding the census statistics and the inconsistencies in listing free persons and slaves, drawing conclusions from the given statistics is unreliable.

Another source of information about photographers is the business directory from individual city directories. Before 1910 most of these directories differentiated between races by indicating a black person with an asterisk or the letter "c" next to the name. But not all city directories used this method, for various reasons. For example, in Oregon, which was not a proslavery state, city directories did not list names by race. (Historians may be quick to say that this was because the state of Oregon did not differentiate between races. But there was a law that stated that free blacks were not allowed to move into Oregon, and the blacks who did live in the state were not allowed to live in the big cities. Hence, they were confined to the rural areas.)

The first documented evidence of a black woman in photography comes from an 1866 Houston directory. As there were no other directories of any kind published there before that year, it is difficult to determine the number of free blacks who worked in Houston before 1866. Mary E. Warren is listed in the 1866 directory with the abbreviation "col." next to her name. Her occupation is listed as a photograph printer and her address was Main between Preston and Prairie. As seen from the 1866 map of Houston (See below), Mary Warren's address is right in the heart of the business district, two blocks from City Hall.

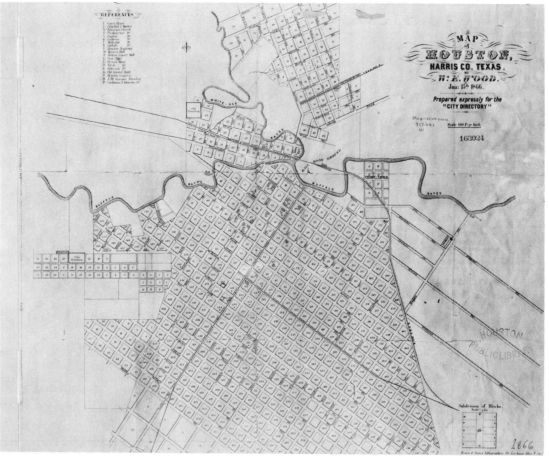

In looking at advertisements in *The Houston Tri-Weekly Telegraph,* the newspaper of the period, and in looking also at the addresses of other photographers living and working in Houston at the time, it is apparent that the building where Mary Warren is listed was a central location for photographic studios and services. T. G. Patrick, C. N. Bean, Blessings Photographic Gallery, and Barr and Wright Photographers were all white photo establishments listed on Main between Preston and Prairie.[23] Mary Warren may have worked for one of these businesses; or did she have a printing service of her own and was not able to advertise it? After all, this was in Texas, which had been a slave state since its first cargo of slaves arrived in 1821. Even though President Lincoln issued the Emancipation Proclamation on January 1, 1863, Texas did not experience Emancipation until June 19, 1865. This date was referred to as "June Teenth" day, and was, for many years, celebrated by blacks in Texas as their Fourth of July. Along with the great many other obstacles that blacks in Houston encountered, no free blacks were allowed to live within the city limits. Few blacks were listed in city directories in Texas, even though four years later, in 1870, the census reported that thirty-nine percent of the population of Houston was black.

It is not known how or where Mary Warren learned her craft; but considering the photographic techniques of that period, she must have received at least some formal or one-on-one training. If she was a slave, she could have learned her craft from her slave owner. But in order to be listed in the city directory, while being black and a woman, her work must have been respected and taken seriously.

There are no records in Texas that give evidence of what happened to Mary Warren or to the work that she did. Nothing tells of her life before or after 1866. She is not listed again in later city directories, nor is she listed in the census directory. But many tragedies occurred in Texas, one of the worst being the September 1867 yellow fever epidemic, in which scores of blacks and whites died.

No record exists in the marriage bureau that Mary Warren changed her name. She must have been an unusual person. She was a Southern black woman, working in a profession unusual for black or white, male or female, in an unusually conservative and prejudiced part of America.

Advertisements in newspapers and periodicals are another major source of information, and they provide a good idea about the professions that black Americans pursued in the nineteenth century. More than twenty newspapers were published by blacks in America between 1832 and 1852. John B. Russworm and Samuel Cornish began the first Afro-American newspaper, *Freedom's Journal,* which lasted three years, from 1827 to 1830, in the state of New York. By 1886, there were 146 newspapers published and edited by blacks in America.

Advertisements for photographic services began appearing in black newspapers as early as 1860. Photographers advertised their abilities as lensmen and also as printers who offered quick, quality work. Photographic printers were as valued as photographers themselves because of the difficult techniques involved in the processing in that era. For example, the collodion process, invented in 1851, was the standard process for photographic printing. It was a technique for making negatives on glass. Collodion was a sticking liquid that was spread onto a glass plate and coated with light-sensitive chemicals. The plate, exposed while wet, required immediate development because the light-sensitive chemical lost its potency as it dried. This is why it was called the "wet plate" process. The fact that these photographic plates had to be exposed and developed immediately made the photographs a remarkable achievement. The collodion process required that photographers concern themselves not only with the composition of their work but also with the messy process they had to undertake in order to see their results. The collodion process remained standard until the introduction of the "dry plate" process in 1880.

The increase in photographic advertisements in black city newspapers can probably be attributed to the increase in the black population of the cities from 1860 to 1900. The black population's migration from the rural areas to the large Southern cities increased by over ninety percent during 1860 to 1870 alone.[24] The chief reasons for blacks' moving to urban areas were economic: to get or find work; to secure better wages or more money; or else they had moved from other cities or from rural areas with their former employers.[25]

Commercial centers in urban areas grew because of the increasing wants and needs of the wealthy classes. Certainly there was an increased demand for photographic services. The black photographer's own clients were largely of his or her own race, but the great demand for photographs in the white community put strains on the white photographers, who were forced to hire black labor to fulfill the demands.

Whites too were advertising in the black newspapers. In *The Concordia Eagle,* Frank Leslie advertised that his *Historical Register* (See Illus. #4) was the only history of the Centennial Exhibition of 1876 written. The ads listed information on photographers and photography and clearly showed that whites felt there was a market for photographic books and information in the black communities.

4. *1877 advertisement for Frank Leslie's* Historical Register

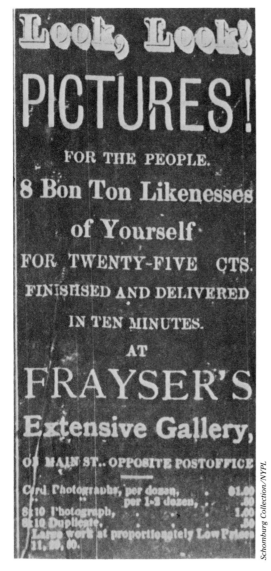

5. 1880 advertisement

At about this time, an article published in *English Woman's Review,* entitled "Coloured Women of America" and dated January 15, 1878, clearly showed the interest of the white female community in the growing black community. The article commended black women for their work in the home and for the leadership they provided within their families. Still, black women's occupations were not counted or noted in the government census. The 1870 census recorded that in all photographic establishments, there were 452 women employed in twenty-eight states. Two hundred and twenty-eight females were recorded as daguerreotypists or photographers, but there was no racial breakdown given.[26] By 1870, photography had become so popular that there were more than three hundred photo galleries in New York City alone.[27]

In the 1880s, more and more photographers were advertising in Negro newspapers around the country. In an issue of one black newspaper, *The Virginia Star* in Richmond, dated March 27, 1880, Frayser's Extensive Gallery advertised "Bon-Ton likenesses of yourself for twenty-five cents" (See Illus. #5) and also promised eight-by-ten photographs for one dollar each, which during the 1880s was a relatively reasonable price. There must have been a great demand and a lot of business, because these ads continued to run week after week.

With the introduction of the "dry plate" process in 1880, which marked the advent of the mass appeal of photography, photographers were no longer tied to their darkrooms. Almost all photographers used this process. Amateurs as well as professionals began to experiment with it. Photography became commercialized. Hand-held cameras were introduced and the photo-finishing industry was born.

Another sign of the commercialization of photography was the numerous articles that ran in *The New York Times.* Although none of these articles referred to blacks in the field, there were some references to blacks as patrons. In one 1885 article, there was mention of black women at a studio on New York's Bowery. The studio was open on Sundays, and most of its clients were clerks and shopgirls who could visit only on their day off. The proprietor of the studio was queried, "Do colored people patronize you much?" and the proprietor responded, "Oh, colored folks sometimes sit for us. I have known colored ladies to sit for tintypes and they ask me why I didn't put a little more rouge on their cheeks."[28]

While the popularity of photography during this period seems to have soared, so did the controversy surrounding it. In a *New York Times* article from 1884, it was implied that ever since the announced invention of the "dry plate" process, offering new and "simpler" techniques for making and developing photographs, there had also been an increase in the number of insanity cases in hospital wards, where patients were found raving about "developers" and "toning baths." With the invention of the "dry plate" process, scores of new instruments and apparatus were developed, increasing the public's confusion as to the correct techniques for making successful pictures.[29] Now that the word "ease" had been introduced into the increasingly popular field of photography, more and more people, even those who had very little knowledge of photography, were drawn into the market. Hence, *The New York Times* article suggested that the insane asylums were filled with these frustrated amateurs.

As a result of the controversy surrounding the number of amateurs in the field, other articles described how photography was being used for blackmailing purposes by both men and women.[30] These "intruders" gave photography a new label: "aggressive." An 1883 *New York Times* article entitled "Photographed While Kissing" relates the story of a young woman who convinced a young cleric to visit her home because she had a private and personal confession to reveal.[31] On his arrival, she revealed that she was in love with him but respected his lifelong dedication to celibacy, whereupon she requested only one kiss from him to console her passion; he complied. A few days later, the cleric received a neatly wrapped parcel containing photographs of himself kissing the

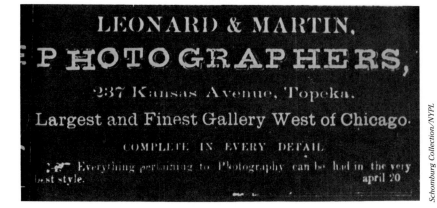

6. *1882 advertisement*

distraught young lady and a note from her explaining that there were eleven more copies, which he could purchase for twenty dollars apiece. She suggested in her note that if he did not want the pictures, she would dispose of them in another manner; negotiations on the matter proceeded.

Many black newspapers continued to carry more and more photography advertisements in the 1880s (See Illus. #7 & 8). Though most of these advertisements were placed by men, two black females were the exceptions. The first was noted in a listing in *The Cleveland Gazette* of May 22, 1886.[32] Fanny J. Thompson of Memphis, Tennessee, was listed as an aspiring photographer. Other articles in different issues of the *Gazette* stated that Fanny Thompson was a noted musician and composer. In fact, a musical piece that she composed, "Fond Memories," was published by the *Gazette*. (Thompson was also mentioned on the society pages of the *Gazette*.) The piece written about her in 1886 mentioned that she would "devote her school vacation to the study of photography"[33] (See Illus. #9).

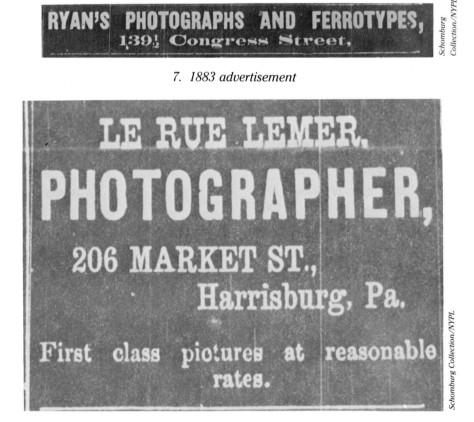

7. 1883 advertisement

8. 1884 advertisement

The other black woman advertiser was Hattie Baker of Cleveland, Ohio, who was most active in 1887 working as a specialist in photographic enlargements. She placed an ad in the *Gazette,* with a paragraph in the column next to the ad stating, "Your attention is called to the advertising of Mrs. Hattie Baker who enlarges photographs."[34]

In 1890, women began to be recognized as serious contributors to photography, both as amateurs and as professionals. The 1890 census listed 2,201 female photographers. This was also the first year that black women photographers were listed separately in the census. Prior to 1890, black women's occupational statistics were lumped into the "other" category, which also included women with Asian and "miscellaneous" backgrounds. The 1890 census listed six Negro women photographers but included no state-by-state breakdown or any other statistical information.[35] This scant statistic became the first evidence of black women being seriously accepted as professional photographers in America.

Blacks were represented in every business listed in the 1890 census schedule. It was also the first year that a distinction was made in the race and color of workers. It showed that, of 975,530 black women employed, only 2.76 percent were employed in manufacturing and mechanical pursuits (the category in which photographers were listed).[36]

two Deputy Sheriffs, the Representative, six Justices of the Peace and seven Constables are all colored.

Miss Fanny J. Thompson, a noted musician and composer of Memphis, whose "Fond Memories" was published by the editor of THE GAZETTE, will devote her school vacation to the study of photography.

The heirs of L. Toussaint L'Ouverture, the great leaders of the slaves in their revolt in San Domingo, are sueing the Girard heirs for money that had

Schomburg Collection/NYPL

9. *1886 society page listing*

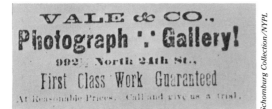

10. 1890 advertisement

11. 1890 advertisement

12. 1899 advertisement

The controversy surrounding women's involvement in photography was focused totally in the white community, as evidenced in the many articles and reports of the time. For example, an article in the October 17, 1890, edition of *Outing* magazine praised women who were interested in pursuing photography.[37] The author, Margaret Bisland, stated: "Women have always been involved in some important capacity in the photographic establishment." She also predicted that the great photographers in American society would be women because they finally had a respected and legitimate medium through which to express their artistic talents, and they possessed the instincts that were necessary to produce quality photographs.

The male authors of photography articles in the same period echoed women's theories about women in photography. In a *Cosmopolitan* magazine piece of March 1893 entitled "Women Experts In Photography," author Clarence Moore wrote: "Unlike the gun, the racquet and the oar, the camera offers a field where women can compete with men upon equal terms."[38] The article also cited the progress women had made in photography and their inclusion as equals in the photographic societies, as evidenced in July 1892, when women were admitted to the photographic convention of Great Britain.

Although publicity was beginning to surround women as photographers, and even though some articles did mention women who were award-winning photographers and exhibition participants, women still were not as recognized as their work merited. The success of women photographers at the time was attributed to women's taste for beauty in composition, which was assumed to be innate; to the belief that women had more leisure time than men to practice; and, for child photography, to women's greater experience with every phase of child life. Most women who were considered competent and successful in artistic photography were married. It was the single woman who pursued the craft for money, professionally.

Around 1892, the cost of purchasing a camera, lens, tripod, and film, with a supply of developing and printing materials, was about ten dollars, which was considered an affordable price by most standards. A *New York Times* article of 1893 quoted slightly higher prices, but investment in a camera outfit was still considered affordable. Said the *Times* article: "It is no longer an unusual or uncommon thing to see a camera in the hands of a woman."[39] Although there were many articles in various magazines describing women's involvement in photography, black publications did not even mention black women photographers.

The inclusion of information and statistics in articles on black photographers can probably be attributed to Booker T. Washington's National Negro Business League, organized in August 1900. Although some statistics were found in the last years of the nineteenth century, no particular recognition was given to the number of creative black participants. With the organization of the League, reports on blacks in business finally came into focus.

In a financial survey of black business transcripts, the League pointed out that blacks were represented in every business that was listed in the 1890 census. The total number of black business persons listed as employed in the 1890 census was 20,020; this number included 190 photographers. There was even mention of a photographer in St. Paul, Minnesota, who was making the incredible sum of $20,000 a year.[40]

The January 27, 1900, issue of *The Kansas City Observer* reported that photographs by black women were to be exhibited in the Paris Exposition of 1900.[41] The U. S. Commission to the Exposition had designated space for a Negro exhibit in an attempt to show the advancement of the black race, and a portion of the exhibit featuring the work of black women included a photography exhibition.

The 1900 census began to give some concrete statistics on the black woman photographer.[42] The report listed a state-by-state breakdown for the women photographers: Illinois two, Massachusetts one, New York two, Ohio two, Pennsylvania one. The statistical report also included information on marital status. It listed nine black women photographers as single, six married, and two widowed. Two of these women were unemployed at the time, but the census listed photography as their profession. But still, out of the 3,587 women photographers listed, only seventeen were black.

The Twentieth Century Union League, a black organiza-

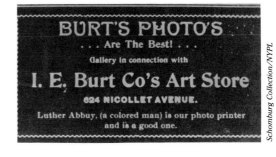

13. *1899 advertisement*

14. *1899 advertisement*

tion in Washington, D.C., published a directory of that area in 1901.[43] Of the number of business persons listed, three were photographers. The League reported that the economic climate for blacks in Washington was healthy for their businesses: there were a large number of black patrons.

Nonblack publications were still focusing on women photographers, pointing out that they were being well paid for their services. Women photographers were working for newspapers, magazines, and photographic journals throughout the country, but again these articles did not make reference to black women.

In 1902, however, *The Colored American* magazine published an article by W. W. Holland entitled "Photography for Our Young People."[44] The article, though the title does not state it, encouraged the participation of black women in the photographic field. The author wrote that although he knew photography to be popular in the black community, the blacks involved in the field were so scattered that he had not yet seen or heard of one black woman photographer. The article described photography as being inspiring and of "financial worth to its master." Because the profession was still in its infancy, black women were being encouraged to grow with it.

Holland also stated that the acquisition of good photographs by blacks was difficult at white galleries because whites did not solicit black patronage. He encouraged black women to get involved in the business to solicit potential black patrons.

Holland probably revealed the general feeling of society toward women in photography, and women themselves raised many objections to photography, saying it was "too expensive" or "too much trouble." The author quotes a woman who was offered a photography outfit as a present as having said, "Oh, I cannot bother with a tripod and a camera. I need my hands to hold up my skirts!" Although many women felt that the cumbersome equipment was not suited for their lifestyle, others did not.

Fannie B. Williams, addressing black women in a 1905 article, wrote: "That the term 'colored girl' is almost a term of reproach in the social life of America is all too true, she is not known and hence is not believed in, she belongs to a race that is best designated by the term 'problem' and she lives beneath the shadow of that problem which envelops and obscures her. The 'colored girl' may have character, beauty, and charms ineffable, but she is not in vogue."[45] This was an accurate description of attitudes toward black women during the 1900s, and it was probably these attitudes that kept black women photographers, amateur or professional, out of the social and professional mainstream that could have appreciated their photographic talent.

Many of the white publications boasted of the new white women photographers entering the profession. One was Frances Benjamin Johnston. Around the same time, Booker T. Washington's National Negro Business League Convention of 1904 listed Mary E. Flenoy as its first black female photographer member, and the only photographer to attend the meeting held in Indianapolis that year.[46] Mary Flenoy was from Danville, Illinois, and was also listed as a member in attendance in 1905, when the League held its meeting in New York City.[47]

Frances Benjamin Johnston, a white photographer who was born to wealthy parents in 1864, traveled easily between two worlds. Her greatest work as a photographer was in 1899, when Booker T. Washington invited her to do a series of photographs of Hampton Institute. These pictures were so successful that she was commissioned a second time by Washington in 1902 to do a series of photographs of Tuskegee Institute and its people; and she did another series in 1906.[48] Johnston photographed black students who represented the best hopes that blacks had for any advancement in segregated America.

Why would Booker T. Washington hire a wealthy white woman photographer to photograph black America's most well-known schools at a time when black photographers such as Tuskegee's own C. M. Battey, or Arthur P. Bedou, or Mary E. Flenoy were more than capable of completing the same assignment? Certainly it would have been beneficial to a black photographer's business, in terms of both money and recognition. In a letter from Frances Benjamin Johnston to Booker T. Washington, Johnston confirmed that she had received $1,000 and the living expenses for both herself and her assistant for over a period of six weeks.[49] She was offered the same terms for Tuskegee as she received for the Hampton job and again was paid $1,000 plus expenses. A thousand-dollar payment was a phenomenal price in 1899, 1902, and 1906. It was an unheard-of sum to pay a black photographer.

Surely Booker T. Washington must have known that there were several capable and talented black male and female photographers who could have handled the same assignment. But assuredly he knew that an accepted, well-recognized photographer would bring proper recognition to the schools; to have hired a white woman photographer was controversial in itself.

The assignment did not escape without a racial incident. One of Johnston's assignments was to photograph the Ramer, Alabama, school, as an example of the spread of the Tuskegee idea.[50] An attractive thirty-six-year-old woman, Frances Johnston, accompanied by George Washington Carver, was met by a black professor, Nelson Henry, on her arrival at Ramer. They proceeded by wagon toward Henry's house. A number of white townspeople, who had gathered to watch Henry's action with his visitor, apparently decided that he had violated the unwritten law of association with a white woman. One of the young men drew a pistol and fired three shots at Henry, who was forced to flee. George Washington Carver helped Johnston to go to a nearby town. Henry was run out of Ramer, escaping to Montgomery. Mobs roamed the streets of Ramer. Other teachers at the Ramer school also fled, and the school collapsed. The photographer threatened to have her friend President Theodore Roosevelt intervene in the Ramer school incident, and she visited the Governor of Alabama to seek his aid for the beleaguered Henry. When things calmed down, Henry moved to another town and opened another school. This was all much more controversial than what Booker T. Washington had had in mind in promoting the positive exposure of famous black institutions. But there would have been little or no attention paid to the schools if a black photographer had been hired to do the same job, even though Booker T. Washington was an advocate of black business. Frances Benjamin Johnston's photographs were carefully executed, with a beautiful but formal interpretation of the scenes she saw, and her employer was very pleased with the results. But the unfortunate fact that a black photographer was not given the opportunity for the assignment only reinforces just how difficult a situation black male and female photographers faced as they pursued success and acceptance in photographic history.

Although black men did much better financially in the photography business than women, it was still a battle royal for any black business to survive. Patronage by black people, who had small purchasing power because of their low-paid occupations, was limited, and black businesses faced competition from white firms with larger capital, more extended credit, and greater business experience. Another problem stemmed from the tremendous effect of white purchasing power on black business, because in many lines of business white people would not patronize blacks at all. The idea that white people would not trade with blacks to any considerable extent and that blacks had to depend upon their own people was steeped into black business persons' minds.[51]

At the end of the first decade of the twentieth century, there was a positive note that indicated the progress to come. The 1910 census showed that the number of Negro women photographers had more than doubled in ten years.

Mary E. Flenoy

Mary E. Flenoy, a black woman, was listed as a member present at the Fifth Annual National Negro Business League Convention, held in Indianapolis in August 1904. She was also listed as a member present at the League's Sixth Annual Convention, held in New York City in August 1905. In both years, her address was listed on the members' roster as 613 South Street, Danville, Illinois. Her profession was listed as a photographer. According to the records from the convention of 1904, Mary Flenoy was the only photographer to have attended the meeting. There were three other members in other professions from Danville present at the convention in Indianapolis, which was not very far from Danville. But in 1905, when the convention was held in New York City, over eight hundred miles east of Danville, Mary Flenoy attended as the only representative from Danville.

The Danville city directories of 1899, 1903, 1904, 1905, and 1906 all list Mary E. Flenoy as a photographer, although in some years she was listed at a different address (See Illus. #15 & 16). There is no evidence to be found of her work. Unfortunately, the loss of the many photographs and work by black photographers was a common thing. Aside from the importance that black photographers held in their own communities, their work carried little or no recognition or importance to anyone outside their own backyard. Not only did the outside world not consider their pictures important; they themselves attached no significance, other than the business transaction of the sale of the photograph, to their own work. More than likely, Mary Flenoy's pictures were discarded, but

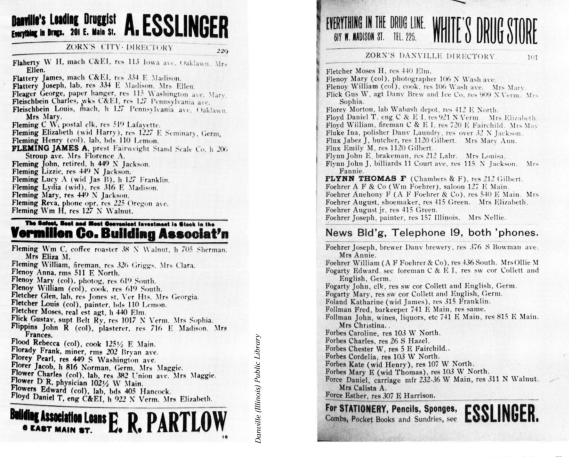

15. Danville City Directory, 1899. Mary E. Flenoy, photographer

16. Danville City Directory, 1906. Mary E. Flenoy, photographer

one hopes they may have been handed down through family members of her patrons. No one in Danville today has ever heard of Mary Flenoy or has any sense of a black woman in 1899 with a camera in her hand.

There is one possible clue as to how she became a photographer. The Danville city directories of 1886 and 1887 list Mary E. Flenoy, "colored," as a domestic living at 122 North Pine Street. This was also the address of one of Danville's wealthiest white citizens, Joseph G. English, a banker, landowner, and at one time the mayor. Unfortunately, quite a few of the city directories for Danville in the 1880s and 1890s are missing. But according to the ones that exist, Mary Flenoy worked as a domestic for the English family at least until

1893. Many white businessmen taught their servants and domestics skills in the production of certain types of goods. The possibility exists that Mary Flenoy learned her photographic skills while working at the English home.

According to the 1899 city directory, Mary Flenoy was married to William Flenoy, who worked as a cook at the popular Palace Restaurant in Danville. They were listed as living at 106 North Washington Avenue. Her photographic studio was located in the heart of the business district, on land owned by the English family. The Flenoys were not listed in the 1890, 1900, or 1910 census. They are also not found in marriage, birth, death or will of records for Vermillion County; nor are they in the lists compiled from the headstones of the cemeteries in the area.

Few blacks lived in the city of Danville proper. Most lived in South Danville or Grape Creek. Grape Creek was a coal mining community, and many of the miners either were black or were white immigrants from Sweden. In Danville itself there was a black preacher, a mail carrier, a day laborer, a domestic, a barbershop owner, a porter, and a washerwoman. These were not all of the blacks in Danville but rather a representation of the kind of work available for blacks at that time in that city. Certainly, the work of Mary E. Flenoy, photographer, was very different.

Part 2

HISTORICAL OVERVIEW

1910–1930

Crisis magazine/NAACP

17. 1910 advertisement for Jennie L. Welcome

In 1910, blacks in the United States represented 10.9 percent of the total American population.[52] While there had been an increase in population for both blacks and whites, the increase for whites was much greater because of the immigration of many Europeans. The census of 1910 listed 404 black photographers and 31,257 white photographers.[53] Census reports from a few states numbered women photographers by race. These states were: Pennsylvania, with five black women photographers; Ohio, with four; Illinois, with four; New York, with two; Michigan, with one; and Massachusetts, with one.[54] There are no other statistical breakdowns indicating the cities, names, or ages of any of these women.

In many of the Northern cities, blacks began to establish their own businesses in increasing numbers. It was during this time that Jennie Louise Welcome, under the name Mme. E. Toussaint Welcome, ran an ad in a 1910 issue of *Crisis* magazine that listed her as the proprietor of a studio in Harlem and as "the foremost female artist of the race"[55] (See Illus. #17). She was born Jennie Louise Van Der Zee on January 10, 1885, in Lenox, Massachusetts. Her parents, John and Susan (Brister) Van Der Zee, were maid and butler to General Grant. Jennie was educated at Lenox High School and took private instruction in art and music in Pittsfield, Massachusetts. The famed Harlem photographer James Van Der Zee was her brother.

On January 10, 1910, Jennie married Ernest Toussaint Welcome, and they moved into a brownstone in New York City where she opened her studio and school for the arts, The Toussaint Conservatory of Art and Music. Over 30 percent of married black women were employed in some capacity during the time, but Jennie was unusual in that she was the black proprietor of an establishment in Harlem that catered to the black community at a time when many of the residents of Harlem were affluent whites. Prior to 1915, 80 percent of employed black women worked in domestic or personal service; few women were business owners or co-owners, and even fewer worked in photography.[56] Later Jennie and her husband moved their business to a house on Long Island.

Blacks were engaged in a variety of occupations at the start of World War I in 1914. A Department of Labor survey stated that the war presented black women with "occupations not heretofore considered within the range of their possible activities."[57] Blacks began to move away from those jobs traditionally assigned to them, and black women were leaving the ranks of domestic service as new jobs opened up for them.

Meanwhile, a group called The Photo-Secession, which had been founded by photographer Alfred Stieglitz in 1902, stated that its goals were "to hold together those Americans devoted to pictorial photography, . . . to exhibit the best that has been accomplished by its members or other photographers, and above all, to dignify that profession until recently looked upon as a trade."[58] Yet, no black photographers were members of this group, nor did they exhibit in the group's shows or galleries. There is little doubt, though, that black photographers showcased work that deeply reflected the life of the people of black America. Black photographers' primary concerns were for income, family support, and business advancement; established white photographers like Stieglitz and Edward Steichen were independently wealthy. Black photographers were also concerned to pose their black subjects in ways that reflected dignity and personal pride. Photographs of blacks by white photographers were generally much less particular about this.

The end of World War I signaled the start of the disintegration of accepted conventions and traditional rules of composition in photography and art. A search for new ways of expression began. White American photographers' thirst for change was due partly to new photographic techniques that were seen throughout Europe, the womb of photography.[59] Yet there remained constant attempts to continue creating an American art separate from European art.

By 1920, the U. S. Census Bureau listed 608 black photographers; 101 of them were black females—the number had more than doubled since the previous census.[60] While there were a total of some 34,259 white photographers in 1920, the number of white women photographers had increased from 4,964 in 1910 to 7,119 in 1920. The Census Bureau reported that the spurt of women photographers between 1910 and 1920 was probably due to the demand for them during World War I, although there were no official women photographers employed by the military. An article published in *The American Journal of Sociology* in March 1930 stated that black businesses were most successful in the South, mainly because of segregation and the need for blacks to establish their own outlets for goods and services.[61]

At a national convention of the National Negro Business League in 1903, one member had made public the fact that he owed his success as a businessman almost entirely to his wife and that he was sure other members "could truthfully say that they owed more to their wives than to any other one thing for their achievements as businessmen."[62] Fannie Barrier Williams, at the League's 1904 convention, held in Indianapolis, spoke on behalf of the "silent partners" who were always concealed from the public's eye; she said that it was the wives who stood "between the businessman and bankruptcy." She also encouraged black women to "become more important in those larger affairs of life where character and achievements count for more than prejudices and suspicions." Williams encouraged black men to confide in their wives, to respect their judgment, and to encourage their talents and virtues. In doing so, the black man would help make black womanhood a part of "all that is best and most beautiful in the world's conception of an ideal woman."[63]

Black women were increasingly becoming a part of the black businessman's career. Historically, the black man and the black woman suffered similar misfortunes, and the limitations put on their ambitions were similar. Because of the realization of this equality of conditioning and training, black couples were destined to share more intimately in the management of business enterprises. Said Fannie Barrier Williams, "Gentlemen, with this kind of woman in your business, you cannot fail, and without her, you have already failed."[64]

An example of this husband and wife business is seen in several photography studios that started after 1920. The Harleston Studio in Charleston, South Carolina (See Illus. #20), the Roberts' Art Studio in Columbia (See Illus. #18 & 19), South Carolina, and the Teal Portrait Studio in Houston, Texas, were all successfully operating business studios serving their communities.

In 1929, Negro women showed the highest rate of employment of any racial group.[65] The crash of 1929, however, set them back. The competition for work set all employable people back, and since blacks were just breaking ground in many industries, they would be the first to go during the economic crisis. Black women, who had always worked to help support their families, lost their jobs, and because of the racial situation in the country, whites were more apt to hire whites if there was a job available. Positions now became very competitive, especially for black women.

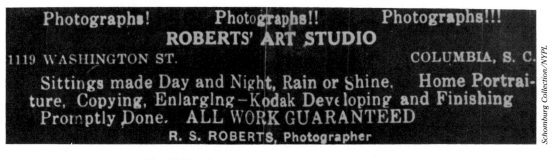

18. 1921 advertisement, Wilhelmina Roberts

19. 1921 advertisement, Wilhelmina Roberts

... The Harleston Studio ...

Portraits

From file or from photographs, Oil Painting, Pastel, Charcoal, Crayon

Free Hand Machine Enlargements

Highest Artistic Standards

Write for circular and out-of-town sittings

118 Calhoun Street   **CHARLESTON, S. C.**

EDWIN A. HARLESTON

Edwin A. Harleston was born in Charleston, South Carolina. Graduated at Atlanta University, A. B. 1904. Studied 1906-1912 at the school of the Museum of Fine Arts, Boston, Mass: Department of drawing and painting under William M. Paxton, Phillip Hale, William Benson and Edmund C. Tarbell specialized in portrait and figure painting.

During the past ten years Mr. Harleston has executed commissions for portraits in many cities throughout the eastern half of the United States.

In the spring of 1922 he equipped and opened up the "Harleston Studio," at Charleston, combining in a most unique way a photograph studio, managed by his wife, Elsie F. Harleston, and a painting studio, conducted by the artist who is generally regarded as the foremost portrait painter of his race in America.

Schomburg Collection/NYPL

20. 1923 advertisement for The Harleston Studio

Elise Forrest Harleston

21. The Photographer

Edwina Harleston Whitlock

In Charleston, South Carolina, in the 1920s, the black professional class served the demands of the black community well, and one of its businesses was a husband and wife portrait studio. It was in the spring of 1922 that Edwin and Elise Harleston opened their Harleston Studio at 118 Calhoun Street in Charleston, combining a painting studio, run by Edwin, and a photography studio, run by Elise.

The couple had first met in Charleston, where they lived and worked. Edwin's brother was married to Elise's sister at the time, which afforded the artistic couple the opportunity to visit each other with some frequency. But Edwin, wanting to further his studies in painting, soon left Charleston to study abroad. Before leaving, he asked Elise to enroll in a photography class so that on his return they could be married and open a studio together. The plan was that he would be the portrait painter and she would be the photographer.

In September 1919, Elise enrolled at the E. Brunel School of Photography in New York City, where it was arranged for her to board in the home of Mr. and Mrs. Robert Elzy, who lived in Brooklyn and were friends of Edwin's. In a letter that Elise wrote to Edwin shortly after the start of her classes, she told of being one of only two blacks that attended the photo school, and that she was the only female student.[66] On finishing her program, she was a competent photographer. But Edwin sensed in Elise much more latent talent, and as he was still away most of the time, he insisted that she enroll at Tuskegee Institute in Alabama. It was there, in 1921, that Elise took graduate courses in photography with C. M. Battey, who was head of the Photographic Division.[67]

When Edwin and Elise returned to Charleston after their

respective travels, they were married as planned and opened a studio. Because Edwin often painted portraits, he began to use Elise as his personal portrait photographer. Instead of having his subjects sit motionless for hours to be painted, he would simply have Elise "freeze" an image of them in a photographic portrait and then he would work directly from her photographs. This pleased his clients, for it saved them many hours of posing.

The technique of painting from photographs was well established by this time and widely accepted in art circles. In Europe, many of the impressionist painters had practiced photography before they became painters. The work of painters Edgar Degas, Pierre Bonnard, and Edouard Vuillard was influenced by photography. Edouard Manet often painted from photographs taken by his friend Felix Nadar. Certainly Edwin Harleston's trip abroad widened the scope of his painting enough that he and Elise ran a successful portrait studio together. Historically, much acclaim was given to Edwin Harleston's painting, and in some cases it was even noted that he was a photographer; but little mention was made of Elise's contribution to their portrait studio.

23. *Edwin Harleston, the painter. Elise Harleston, photographer*

22. *1922, The Harleston's Building which housed the Harleston studio. Elise Harleston, photographer*

*24. The Harleston Studio
Greeting Card. Elise Harleston,
photographer*

*25. Unidentified portrait.
Elise Harleston,
photographer*

*26. Elise's Sister. Elise Harleston,
photographer*

*27. A painting of Elise's sister by Edwin
Harleston, painted from Elise's photograph.*

28. *Old Man "Scout." Elise Harleston, photographer*

29. Unidentified woman in portrait. Elise Harleston, photographer

Edwina Harleston Whitlock

Edwina Harleston Whitlock

*30. Market woman. Elise Harleston,
photographer*

*31. Chimney sweep. Elise Harleston,
photographer*

Edwina Harleston Whitlock

32. Landscape. Elise Harleston, photographer

Wilhelmina Pearl Selena Roberts

33. *The Photographer*

Collection of Wilhelmina Wynn

Wilhelmina Pearl Selena Williams married Richard Roberts, a photographer from Fernandina, Florida, in 1902, when she was nineteen. They made their home and studio in Columbia, South Carolina. Wilhelmina learned from her husband the mechanics of the camera; she enjoyed reading books about photography but had no other formal training. She was Richard Roberts's assistant, and although she never declared that she would go out and take somebody's photograph, she did tend to the studio while her husband worked at his income-producing job as a custodian in downtown Columbia. Her specialty became photographing babies. She liked to talk and she liked to laugh. She enjoyed the walk up and down the hill to their studio, six blocks from their home at 1119 Washington Street, just west of Main Street. The area housed several black businesses: N. H. Collins's Merchant Tailor Shop; Dr. A. B. Johnson's office; The Green Leaf Café; Jake Eubanks's Shoe Repair Shop; The Count Drug Store; two theaters; and Johnson's Funeral Home. Ninety-five percent of the patrons of the Roberts' Art Studio were black.

Wilhelmina had a wide knowledge of fabrics, and she was also an excellent seamstress. She had a great sense of detail, and she often contributed greatly to the appearance of her clients by changing the styles of the clothing.

She was a mother devoted to her eight children, and she was also very active in the church. She would prepare hot biscuits and grits for her family every morning for breakfast, seven days a week, and she was an excellent cook.

At a penitentiary not too far from the Roberts home, Wilhelmina would see the chain gangs, made up mostly of black prisoners, and she would take lemonade out to them. Once, some white prisoners who had just been released from the penitentiary came up the driveway to her home. They asked Wilhelmina for some food and she gave them biscuits.

Wilhelmina taught one of her sons to cook for the family when she was away at the studio. When she and her husband would take trips to cities and towns outside of Columbia, the entire family would travel in an old Dodge touring car. Richard Roberts died in 1936 and Wilhelmina closed the studio and sold the equipment. They had built a close relationship centered on taking pictures. She was always one hundred percent supportive of his work, but she never worked away from home, other than in her studio. She died in 1976 at ninety-three.[68]

34. Wilhelmina Roberts's daughter. Wilhelmina Roberts, photographer

35. Little girl and roses

36. Grandmother with three children. Wilhelmina Roberts, photographer

37. Unidentified woman. Wilhelmina Roberts, photographer

In 1930, the Census Bureau reported that in the United States there were a total of 23,836 white male photographers and 7,427 white female photographers.[70] It also reported 545 black photographers, 85 of whom were female.[71]

The Women's Bureau of the census pointed out that in 1930, 15 out of 100 white photographers were female.[72] Although the number of white photographers far exceeded the number of black photographers, there were 18.4 black female photographers to every 100 black male photographers, a higher number proportionately than the white female to the white male. There is another interesting statistic: From 1900 to 1930, the number of black photographers rose from 247 to 545, an increase of 120 percent.[73]

By 1930, the role of women wage earners had changed dramatically. The Depression led to increased competition for fewer jobs and at the same time created a demand that women become actively involved in the workforce. During the years preceding the Depression, black women and their families had migrated northward in large numbers to seek economic opportunity. They had left the South for various reasons, one being their economically depressed life-styles; now they were faced with the same situation in the North.

In a study conducted by Estelle Hill Scott in 1939 entitled "Occupational Changes Among Negroes in Chicago," photography was listed as a "clean" profession and an occupation in which blacks were heavily represented in 1930.[74] The study listed ten black women photographers in Chicago who represented four percent of the share of photographic work. The blacks who did "clean" work were almost entirely confined to the black neighborhoods and were thus dependent on low-wage earners for their livelihood.

Isolation from white America forced the black community to grow stronger and more self-reliant. Since the needs of the black community were the same as any other community, a solid group of black professionals began to flourish. The Harlem Renaissance, which Alain Locke appraised as giving white America "a general acceptance of the Negro today as a contributor to national culture,"[75] drew large numbers of photographers into Harlem to document conditions there in the 1930s. Harlem had been declared the cultural capital of colored America.[76] Government-sponsored projects such as the Work Projects Administration were directly assisting programs that advanced and aided opportunities for black artists. One photographer, Winifred Hall Allen, managed a photography studio in Harlem and documented much of the Harlem business and social life of the 1930s. Also a successful portrait photographer, she was the best-known black woman photographer working in Harlem.[77] During this period there was also growth in the number of national black professional business directories and magazines. This period also saw the birth of the Farm Security Administration or FSA (1930–1940), a government program in which photography became a powerful weapon for awakening the social consciousness of Americans. There was only one black photographer, Gordon Parks, who worked for the FSA, even though much of the subject matter concerned the state of black America. But there were many capable black photographers who could have filled some of those positions.

In 1936, only three years short of photography's centennial, New York City boasted that there were 1,500,000 cameras in active use there alone, which meant that there was about one camera per family for a population of 7 million. A Kodak market survey showed that the country's largest city, New York, was "the apple of the manufacturer's eye." Compared with the country as a whole, New York City had both more cameras and a highter percentage of film development. The survey also showed 16 million cameras among the national population of 122 million. New York accounted for more than its share of photofinishing, one-seventh of all that was done in the country.[78]

Growth in the photo industry was evident in the many periodicals, magazines, and newspapers that were published by the black community. Black photographers' advertisements showed up more and more, but the most significant increase in ads came after 1939, at the beginning of World War II.

Because a different method of classification was used in the 1940 census, it is impossible to make accurate comparisons with the years between 1930 and 1940. The Depression took a heavy toll on many financial and business enterprises, and as a result the numbers of blacks engaged in business diminished considerably. In 1930, the number of black photographers was listed at 545, as compared with the figure for 1940, which listed only 122 black photographers—a significant decrease in one decade.[79] Photography was hard work and brought a comparatively small return. This, though, was synonymous with the history of black wage earners. Some exceptions were talented black women who were married to successful men and who were allowed some financial freedom to express themselves through photography. Eslanda Cardoza Goode Robeson, wife of Paul Robeson, and Billie Davis, wife of Collis Davis, a chemistry professor at Hampton Institute, both working independently of their spouses, contributed their experiences.

In September 1939, World War II broke out in Europe, one hundred years after the August 9, 1839, public announcement of the invention of photography. The war significantly affected the growth of photography, which played an important role in the war effort.

In May 1942, the Women's Army Corps was established, and it put out a call for healthy women with high school educations. These women would not be involved in combat but would be paid on the same scale as their male counterparts. The first group of thirty-nine black women arrived at Fort Des Moines only to be faced with racial segregation. Their sleeping and eating facilities were separate from those of the white women officer candidates, but all of the women shared the same classroom. The thirty-six black women who graduated were assigned to specific jobs in certain areas; some received jobs as technicians and photographers. Elizabeth Williams, a photographer from Houston, Texas, signed up in 1944 and became an official army photographer, covering all aspects of military life. She was the first black female photographer to attend the Fort Monmouth, New Jersey, Photo School. She graduated with honors, first in her class. She was a pioneer for black women in the military.

The National Security Women's Corp offered photography courses, and the photo labs at the military war colleges and training centers across the country were filled with women photographers. In fact, women in photography flourished as never before, as both amateurs and professionals.

At the Lowry Field near Denver, Colorado, there was a photography class held just for WACs. Many of the women who graduated from these schools were hired to teach photography to their male counterparts.[80] One of the greatest commercial uses for the Women's Air Force Service Pilots was a project such as aerial photography.[81]

Hundreds of amateur women photographers participated in specialized USO work in 1943. The idea of taking servicemen's pictures for their families and hometown newspapers originated in Hempstead, Long Island, when a USO photographic expedition was sent to the servicemen's club. The idea was so popular that it soon became a widespread practice in other parts of the country.[82] American troops listed photographs from home among their favorite gifts.[83]

While the use for and interest in photography grew, civilian photographers were faced with a limited supply of equipment and supplies because of the war. The concerns surrounding the availability of camera supplies were soon realized. Photographers, when making purchases, were confronted with restrictions and were forced to learn to use less equipment, and thus to use more care and skill. At a time when the general public was restricted from picture making, the "Camera Girls" were popularizing snapshots taken in the nightclubs.

During the first few months of 1942, photographic goods were still somewhat available since many stores had on hand a large stock of merchandise. But soon after, there was a decrease of at least fifty percent in camera production, and the cameras produced were conspicuous for their lack of aluminum, brass, copper, and bronze. Glass, wood, and in some cases plastic, were substituted. The marketing of old and unused cameras was popular among dealers, and a plea went out to people to dig cameras out of the attics and trade them in for defense bonds. After overhauling a camera, dealers would then resell it. The photographic retailers felt at the time that the war was going to make people more conscious of photography than any manufacturer, distributor, or dealer ever dreamed of, and that the camera market was just waiting for development.

Photo studios like the Avalon Photography Studio, run by Ruth Washington in Los Angeles (1940), were able to do a good business photographing schools and portrait work. Vera Jackson (See Illus. #47), a California photographer, was covering the black elite, entertainers, and stars of Hollywood and sports for *The California Eagle* newspaper.

By the end of the war, the statistics on women photographers were startling. Whereas in 1940 there had been 4,623

47. Advertisement in The California Eagle. *"Vera Jackson, Photographer"*

women photographers, the number increased to 9,088 in 1950, an increase of 96.6 percent.[84] Census statistics showed that women were represented in all 446 occupational categories because of the more specialized skills they learned during the war.[85]

Photography studios run by black women could be found in major cities all over the country, as evidenced by the listing in the city directories and advertisements in popular black magazines (See Illus. #48, 49, 50, 51). New York, Houston, Los Angeles, and Chicago were all popular places for photo studios, and many of them were run by women. The Vanderbilt Studio (See Illus. #48), in Wilmington, North Carolina, which was managed by Lydia Mayo and Carol Augustus, was one of the studios that advertised.

By 1950, there were more women photographers than in any other decade. Approximately half the families in the United States, about 26 million people, took still photographs, according to a two-year survey by Eastman Kodak's market research department.[86] About ninety percent of the population owned boxed or folding-type cameras, and three out of five camera owners used them regularly. Women were the heaviest purchasers of film, most of which came from drugstores. The survey also showed that the number of camera-owning families with and without children were about equal, but those with children owned forty percent more cameras than the other half; boys and girls from ten to seventeen were more conscious of pictures than ever; teenagers bought about twenty percent of the film used in amateur cameras; and men bought more than seventy-five percent of the film for the more professional, advanced types of cameras.[87]

The 1950 Kodak survey also showed clearly that the war had had a profound effect on photography and on women professionals. Black women had become one-tenth of all employed women, and of the total population of black women, thirty-seven percent were wage earners.[88] Clearly, the contributions of both black and white women in photography were at a peak during the 1940s.

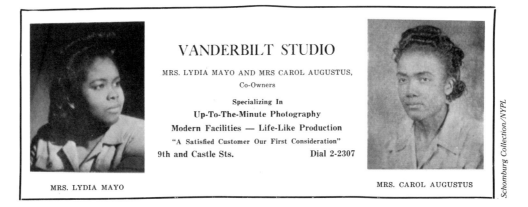

VANDERBILT STUDIO

MRS. LYDIA MAYO AND MRS CAROL AUGUSTUS,
Co-Owners

Specializing In
Up-To-The-Minute Photography
Modern Facilities — Life-Like Production
"A Satisfied Customer Our First Consideration"

9th and Castle Sts.   Dial 2-2307

MRS. LYDIA MAYO   MRS. CAROL AUGUSTUS

48. The Vanderbilt Studio, 1946

E. F. JOSEPH STUDIOS

IN PHOTOGRAPHS ALONE
CAN YESTERDAYS LIVE . . .

DISTINCTIVE WORKMANSHIP . . . DEPENDABLE
SERVICE . . . MINIMUM PRICES . . . is our policy
in serving you.

COMPLETE PHOTOGRAPHIC SERVICE

For an Appointment Soon

Phone OLympic 0246
384 Fiftieth Street, Oakland, Calif.

SILHOUETTE Official Photographer for
Oakland, Berkeley, San Francisco

Audubon 3-0679

WOODARD'S PHOTO SHOP
Wedding Parties and Groups
2386 SEVENTH AVENUE
Second Floor

Bet. 139th and 140th Sts.   New York City

49. Advertisement for Woodard's studio where
Winifred Allen served as an apprentice

THE WOODARD STUDIO

Dallas' Premier Race Studio

Compliments

100 Years of Negro Progress

Where There is Beauty, We Take It
Where There Is None, We Make It

Mrs. E. A. Woodard, Prop.

3415 Howell   Phone 5-7898

50. Emma King Woodard, photographer's ad

51. 1946 advertisement

Winifred Hall Allen

62. Untitled portrait of boy

Winifred Hall Allen

63. Portrait, in a satin dress

Winifred Hall Allen

64. Untitled portrait

Winifred Hall Allen

65. Miss Webster

Winifred Hall Allen

66. A portrait

Winifred Hall Allen

67. Willie Lipsett

Winifred Hall Allen

68. Untitled portrait

Winifred Hall Allen

69. Mr. Baker

70. *Lilac Beauty Shop*

71. Beauticians of the Ritz Beauty Shoppe

72. Mrs. Scott, owner of Ritz Shoppe, seated in front

73. *A hairstyle*

Winifred Hall Allen

74. *A Harlem church choir*

Winifred Hall Allen

75. *Sister Gertrude*

Winifred Hall Allen

76. *First Holy Communion*

• 69 •

Winifred Hall Allen

77. A soldier

Winifred Hall Allen

78. William E. Woodard, photographer, 1936.

Winifred Hall Allen

79. A Garveyite

Winifred Hall Allen

80. Two men looking over papers

81. A.C. Harris, cleaning the Lido Pool on 146th Street

Johnnie Mae Bomar

Johnnie Mae Bomar, from Akron, Ohio, achieved national prominence when she won the Ohio Shriners' beauty contest at Cleveland in 1948 and went on to represent Ohio in the finals. Bomar became a professional photographer in November 1946.

82. Photographer, Johnnie Mae Bomar

Alberta H. Brown

The Browns' Studio, located in Richmond, Virginia, was a family business in which Alberta Brown assisted her husband George Brown in their studio until he became too ill to continue working. Alberta continued to run and operate the studio after her husband died. In the earlier days, she had specialized in hand tinting carefully executed portraits. But although she created some of the studio portraits, most of her work was conducted outside the studio; she took the class pictures for many of Richmond's black schools.

Private Collection

83. The Browns' Studio

Billie Louise Barbour Davis

Collis Davis

84. The Photographer

Born in Kansas City, Missouri, in 1906, Billie Barbour graduated from Sargeant College, now known as Boston University. While studying there she met her husband-to-be, Collis Davis, who was studying organic chemistry at Harvard during the summer. Both completed their studies before their marriage. She earned a degree in physical education at Sargeant, and he earned his degree in chemistry from Columbia University.

The Davises moved to Hampton, Virginia, around 1930. Collis Davis began teaching chemistry and Billie Davis taught dance; both worked at the Hampton Institute. It was during this period that Billie became interested in photography. She learned her photographic skills from Hampton's photography instructor. Billie's close friends and associates at Hampton were not the wives of faculty members; she chose her friends from among the artists who were teaching at Hampton, such as Alex Katz and Ruben Burrell, the photography instructor. Her artistic pursuits may never have been encouraged or stimulated by her female peers at Hampton because they were interested in traditional women's roles. Billie Davis decided that her life, her goals, and her projects were more important, and she never really wandered from that belief.

Although Billie probably started out with a Brownie Kodak, she later came to rely on a Leica and a four-by-five view camera. She also did some 120 2¼-by-2¼ work. She converted a laundry room at home into a darkroom by lining the windows with blackout shades, green on one side and black on the other; this was done during World War II. She painted her walls black and installed a couple of slate sinks.

Billie photographed a wide range of subject matter, but her main interest was portraiture. She did portraits of the various faculty at Hampton, including writer J. Saunders Redding. Billie was often asked to attend birthday parties, celebrations, and other events, to photograph many of the Hampton faculty families. She was popular with the children and spent a lot of time photographing them as well as her own children. She also enjoyed shooting landscapes and skyscapes. Sometime in the late 1940s and early 1950s, and probably influenced by other photographers of the period like Edward Weston, she began doing cloud studies.

Billie took a lot of care in the mounting and presentation of her photographs, yet they rarely surfaced from the carefully constructed portfolio that she made and stored in a sleek black cabinet in her living room at Hampton. It was a rare moment when she would take it out to show someone; this generally happened when good friends came by to visit.

Around 1950, because of a problem with her legs, Billie was forced to stop teaching dance. She began spending more time in the darkroom. It was not uncommon for her children to watch her while she worked. She taught her only son, Collis Jr., the rudiments of the darkroom and how to operate a camera; he has since made photography a career and still uses much of his mother's equipment. Billie began experimenting with photograms, photographic chemistry, and manipulation in the darkroom, without the camera. She experimented with abstract studies, using 3D materials to create flat graphic art. Her portrait work shows clean composition and stark lighting techniques. Clean backgrounds and tight headshots often characterized her portraiture. She often had her subjects looking off camera, off the axis of the lens. She created moods by using a single source of lighting; this play on shadows created strong contrasts in her composition, very much the way Steichen used lighting to create stark, commanding portraits.

In 1955, Billie Davis died of arteriosclerosis, a young artist at the age of forty-nine.

Louise D. Stone

85. Experimental photograph. Billie Davis, photographer

Collis Davis

86. Untitled, from dance series.
Billie Davis, photographer

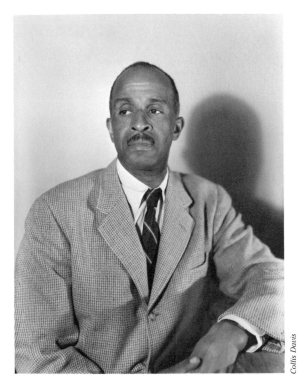

Collis Davis

87. J. Saunders Redding, the writer.
Billie Davis, photographer

Emma Alice Downs

Emma Alice Downs was a WAC staff photographer.

Johnson Publishing Company

88. The Photographer

Camera Girls

On October 23, 1984, an interview was conducted with Charles Williams at his home in Los Angeles. In 1940–46, Williams, a photographer, was the proprietor of several popular nightclubs on Central Avenue, in the black section of Los Angeles. His clubs featured "Camera Girls," who became quite popular and were a major attraction to his nightclub business. Williams was personally responsible for the discovery and training of all his Camera Girls. In the interview, he describes the concept he created and the important role these Camera Girls played.

JMA: What was the concept of a Camera Girl?

CW: Well, during the nightclub period, and that was, of course, during the war, film, cameras, bulbs, many photographic items were very difficult to get. The armed forces took over all of the things that Eastman Kodak and other photo suppliers put out. Even the people who already had cameras couldn't buy film because film and paper for enlarging was made with pure silver, and it was important that those materials and money went into the war effort. They didn't want the public wasting it. Only the war plants got as much film as they needed.

Because of the civilian restrictions on photo supplies, one of the ways that people could get pictures was in the nightclubs. A Camera Girl became the ideal attraction for the nightclub business in taking pictures of the customers. A few professional photographers who set up concessions at nightclubs were able to get enough operating supplies to keep them in business.

JMA: What was a Camera Girl's duty, what was her role?

CW: Her role was to take the pictures. She would walk around the club with her camera and her bag on her shoulder loaded with her film and bulbs, because they used bulbs in those days, and shoot pictures of people who wanted them to show their new girlfriends or their family or just their friends. Most nightclubs would have a darkroom within the club. The Camera Girl, after taking her shot, would take the film back to the darkroom, where it would be processed by the darkroom man and then given back to her. Her main job, then, was to go back and sell the photographs to the people.

JMA: So you mean, even though she would go up to a table and take a photograph, she wasn't guaranteed a sale? She would take the photograph, have it developed, come back, and then try to sell it?

CW: Yes. Quite often, though later on after this era started, the Camera Girls would get the approval of the customers that wanted to buy their pictures first. The customers almost guaranteed that they were going to buy a picture, in so many words, without putting up the money. The Camera Girl didn't really want her customers to put up the money, as the concession owner felt that if the customer paid for one picture, that's all they would buy. So, we would prefer to wait until the Camera Girl came back to the tables with all of these pictures. Perhaps there were five or six people at a table. The Camera Girl would take one picture of the group first. Then she would deliver the film to the darkroom person, who would make up enough pictures for each one in the group. Then the darkroom printer would pair the couples off, either printing individual pictures of a head and shoulder of each person or maybe if the darkroom person could see that this girl was with this fellow, pair them off, by couple. Then they would want that one as much as the whole picture. So you had a good opportunity to sell twenty to thirty dollars' worth of pictures at each table.

JMA: So would you consider a successful Camera Girl someone who took a good photograph or someone who could sell the photograph?

CW: She had to do both. If she didn't take a good photograph in the first place she wasn't going to sell it because the cus-

Winifred Allen

89. The Lido, during WWII

Winifred Allen

90. A night at the Lido Club, New York

tomer wouldn't want it. It was the concessioner's job to get a girl who was personable and who had the patience to learn how to use the camera. We would give her first only the steps that she needed immediately. For instance, if I found a girl who I thought had everything and she wanted a job, I would take her in, put the camera in her hand, fix everything, even pull out the slide, and say, "Now point this at the people, get back far enough so that you can get the whole table when you look through the viewfinder, and just push the button." That's all she had to do and bring it back to the darkroom, and we'd fix it up for her again. Until she was comfortable with the routine. I could make a Camera Girl out of anyone who wanted to do it. Most of the girls I trained had never had a camera in their hands before.

JMA: So you gradually taught them one step at a time?

CW: One step at a time. Very simple. After a couple of days, she was used to routine. The next step was how to put the holder in the camera, how to set the aperture for distances, and how to put the bulb in and load her own camera.

JMA: How much did you charge for pictures, and how much money did the Camera Girls make?

CW: It started out, the whole business of paying the girls, five dollars a night. That was their basic guarantee. And then we charged a dollar and a quarter for one picture and I would give the Camera Girl five cents off of every picture after her sale. A little bit later I started giving her a quarter off of every picture. She got the quarter, we got the dollar. Quite often some of the fellows would give them tips. Not too often; they couldn't depend on sizable tips, but they'd get a few.

JMA: How many nights a week did they work, and what kinds of hours did they work?

CW: They usually worked six nights a week. A nightclub was open every night except Monday, and the camera girls generally started around ten P.M. Every nightclub in town was busy during the war. People had money and no place to go, no place to spend it but nightclubs. We would take pictures right up until closing time, about twenty minutes to two. Nightclubs in California closed at two. Our business really got good about eleven and ran to about one-twenty. If we had good working girls and they knew what they

91. Steppin' out

92. Musician at the Cosmopolitan Social Club

were doing, they would take pictures up to a quarter to two, and have them back to the people before they were ready to walk out at two. The girls had to know how to move and get the pictures in right away, not wasting their time. They had gotten so that they could even take pictures a little later. But of course the nightclub owners didn't want people hanging around after two waiting for pictures, and many of the photographers did that, which just about ruined their business.

JMA: When you think of Cigarette Girls, they were always wearing costumes that were very suggestive or showing the figure. Why wasn't that true with the Camera Girls and what did they wear?

CW: They wore their regular street clothes and we never insisted they wear anything else. Never even thought about it. I never thought about putting them in costumes because, in the first place, that wasn't our reason for having them there. They were there to take pictures for themselves—so we didn't really want the customers to be interested in the girl any more than the fact that she was nice and pleasant and personable. The Cigarette Girls and the others were in costumes and wore short skirts and other things to be attractive because they stood around longer. Our girls didn't have time for that, to be around customers that long. Take a picture and get out of the way and get it to the darkroom, and then get it back and get it sold and get to the next group.

JMA: What was the longevity of Camera Girls? How long would they last?

CW: I had Camera Girls that lasted with me from the time I started until the nightclub business went out, about five or six years. One of the reasons they stayed with me was because during that time you couldn't buy gasoline unless you had stamps, and you couldn't get stamps unless you worked at a defense plant. So people weren't able to drive their cars. If I didn't pick the girls up myself, I would have taxis to pick them up, and I would send them home in cabs if I didn't take them home personally. I treated my Camera Girls like they were really something special to me, like they were important to me.

Ann Elizabeth Jackson

Ann Jackson, who was born in 1922, was the only woman photographer employed by the Veterans Administration in Columbus, Ohio, in the 1950s. Specializing in high-quality copy work, she made reproductions of X-rays and other medical documents, which were shipped to physicians in VA and private hospitals all over the country. An ex-fashion designer and government clerk, Jackson was an assistant photographer specializing in line copy work before joining the VA staff. She also worked as a freelance press and portrait photographer.

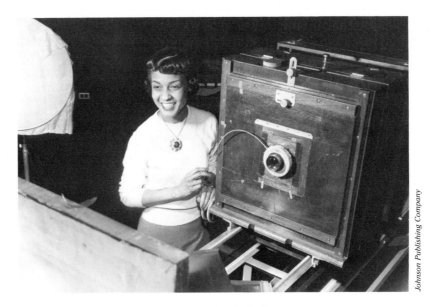

Johnson Publishing Company

93. Ann Elizabeth Jackson

Vera Jackson

Vera Jackson was born in Wichita, Kansas, on July 21, 1912. She remembers her early years as being in a warm and happy environment, until her mother died when Vera was five. After her mother's death, Vera was raised by her father, whom she idolized, and her great-grandmother, who helped them purchase and move to a farm in Corona, California, in the 1920s. Her father was an avid reader and a lover and collector of books. He also took photographs, often carrying his cameras. Vera wanted to follow his pattern. Her fascination with the camera dates from those early childhood years, as a result of her admiration for her father.

In 1930, Vera graduated from Corona High School. In 1931, she married Vernon Jackson and within the next four years they had two sons. In 1936, Vera got her first job, at the Mason Music Company, where she was a "Number Please Girl." A Number Please Girl's job was to play records for patrons at the various juke-boxes on Los Angeles's Central Avenue. Vera remembers: "There were shifts, they changed each week from day shift to swing to graveyard. We learned the numbers for hundreds of records to be played at a moment's notice. We played the wrong numbers often enough and were scolded by our customers."

Around 1936, Vera enrolled in a government-sponsored photography program and learned to use Speed Graphic and other types of cameras, as well as to print and enlarge. She was fond of her teacher George Manuel, who took a lot of time with his students, and especially with Vera, his prize pupil. At the same time, Vera also took classes at Frank Wiggins, a career high school, where she won several prizes

94. The Photographer

for her photographs; one of them appeared on the cover of *The Los Angeles School Journal.* She next worked for a freelance photographer, Maceo Sheffield, as his printer. He was doing freelance work for *The California Eagle,* where she went on a job with him and met its editor, Charlotta A. Bass. Bass eventually hired Vera as a staff photographer. Vera was assigned to work primarily with Jesse Mae Brown, who was the society editor.

Of her tenure at the paper, Vera says: "I was never quite the same. None of us were after coming under the influence of Mrs. Bass. She was way ahead of her time in civil rights. She was fighting first one cause then another before it was popular to do so." Today, Vera appreciates her photographs showing that long ago era.

Vera and social editor Jesse Mae met all the celebrities who came to town. Vera photographed parties and met and took

Photograph by Vera Jackson

95. Mrs. Bass switching on the first stop light on Central Avenue in Los Angeles

pictures of celebrities in the theater, the arts, music, societies, and the sports world. One of Vera's favorite celebrities was Jackie Robinson, the man who broke the color barrier in major league baseball. She met him through his brother-in-law, Chuck Williams, with whom she studied photography at the University of California. Vera photographed Jackie and his wife Rachel at their home in Los Angeles when their first child was born.

Mary McLeod Bethune was on the list of great black Americans whom Vera met and photographed during her early years as a photographer. Photographing and hearing Bethune speak was an experience Vera says she will never forget. While there were many people who were important to Vera and who had a significant influence on her work, she felt especially fortunate to have met and known Dorothy Dandridge. Dandridge, a young and talented actress, was not only a photogenic beauty; she was also a warm and gracious person.

As a press photographer, Vera did feature stories like "The Best Dressed" and "First Achievements By Blacks." She loved the excitement of her work. Working as a press photographer on assignment to get a news or publicity picture that was clear, sharp, and flattering to the subject, and one that would reproduce well, was no easy task. The newsprint and ink used were often substandard. Vera was very much aware of herself and all that was happening around her. She stated, "I firmly believe that our frenzied pursuit of the finest life had to offer was due to the hard times from which many of us had just emerged; we had just come out of the hard luck times of the 1930s. In order to forget these bad times and to look forward to the promise of prosperity and jobs and other opportunities, there was a showiness on the part of most of us. We were most impressed with elegance, richness, or opulence in our homes, and our dress and all activities which we pursued."

Vera was always given a byline, but she was never impressed with a false sense of the importance of her job, and as a consequence she did extremely well. She even taught her husband Vernon what she knew. He bought a Speed Graphic camera, and he too started working professionally.

When *The Los Angeles Sentinel*, another black newspaper, started up, it lured social editor Jesse Mae away. Vera stayed on with *The Eagle* for a while, until her husband strongly suggested that she go back to school and become a schoolteacher. He felt that she could not be a photographer forever, although he also knew that she did not want to stay home and be a housewife.

Vera went back to school, and in three and half years she received her B.A. and began teaching her first classes in art on the elementary school level. She continued to study at night, eventually receiving her Master's degree. During her teaching years, she continued to take pictures, which she sold to several magazines. For the last five years, Vera has been attending Riverside Community College in Riverside, California, studying sculpture, ceramics, and painting.

Vera always wanted to travel and use her photography skills abroad. She went to Africa four times and explored all parts of the continent. She traveled to the Orient and around the world. Her pictures have been shown at the Vernon Library, the Los Angeles County Public Library, the Afro-American Museum of History and Culture in Los Angeles, and the Museum of Art in San Francisco.

While she feels that her press photographs are now in a historical category, Vera believes that the importance of photography comes through what it contributes to mankind, rather than to the arts. "I believe that as in a painting, a photographer can create a mood and tell a story that will involve the viewer and cause him to feel, to understand, or to identify with the picture. A photographer's intent to bring greater understanding and appreciation for the human condition or the world about us, that's what I tried to do with my work; and that in a nutshell is what photography means to me. Learning to see and trying to let the world see what I see.

"Personally, photography has enriched my life in so many ways. It is my way of telling the world how I feel about the beautiful experience of living and learning. It is a wonderful opportunity for self-expression—to bring greater understanding in our own way to help others to understand the human condition and the world as we see it. I'd rather think I am helping to open up new horizons of the mind, rather than to just make beautiful photographs, which, of course, I am also trying to do. If it is art, all well and good, but I hope I am also bringing greater understanding of how we were in the 1930s and 1940s."

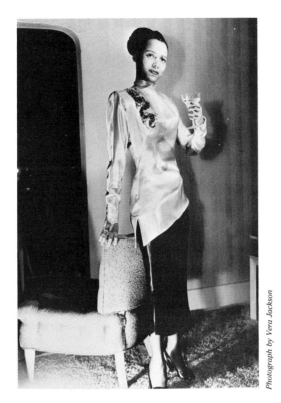

Photograph by Vera Jackson

96. *Dorothy Dandridge*

Photograph by Vera Jackson

97. *Dorothy Dandridge*

Photograph by Vera Jackson

98. *Phillipa Schuyler (*left*) and Hattie McDaniel (*right*)*

Photograph by Vera Jackson

99. *Birthday celebration for Mary McLeod Bethune; Lena Horne standing at far left*

100. Mrs. Charlotta Bass (left), Adam Clayton Powell, Jr. (center),
Hazel Scott (right)

101. Max the printer

Dora Miller

A native of Oklahoma City, Dora Miller came to Los Angeles from New York, where she had been a model. She received a scholarship to study photography at the California Institute of Photography in 1947 in exchange for working as a receptionist in a school charm program. After receiving her certificate, Dora assisted in running the Avalon Photography Studio in Los Angeles with Norman Siminoff, Chuck Williams, and its owner Ruth Washington. Eventually, Dora took over the studio; all of the equipment was leased in her name.

In 1949, Dora married Walter Miller; they were married for three years. She died at the age of thirty-three of a heart attack.

102. The Photographer

Charles Alonzo Williams, Sr., President
California Institute of Graphic Arts at Los Angeles

Eslanda Cardoza Goode Robeson

103. Eslanda in uniform

Eslanda Cardoza Goode Robeson, also known as Essie Robeson, a trained chemist, began studying photography while living in London after her marriage to singer and actor Paul Robeson. Eslanda was a scientist who practiced photography as an avocation. She did not call herself a professional photographer, yet her photographs reveal philosophical ideas, a view of worldly political problems, and deep human compassion. Eslanda also used her photographic talent to illustrate and assist herself in her anthropological fieldwork. She often used photographic note-taking methods to describe situations, especially at times when pencil and paper could not adequately describe her experience.

Eslanda, who had studied in both the United States and England, particularly enjoyed theater and anthropology. Born in Washington, D.C., on December 15, 1896, she came from a family that stressed the need for education. Her father, one of the first blacks to graduate from Northwestern University, died when Eslanda was very young. Her mother worked to earn money to educate Essie and her two brothers. In 1905, they moved to New York and lived in a cold-water railroad flat. Eslanda learned from her mother that education was the most important thing in life. Eslanda's maternal grandfather was educated in Scotland at Glasgow University and founded Avery Institute, the first school for blacks in South Carolina. His name was Francis Lewis Cardoza, and he believed in the importance of blacks' obtaining a good education. In 1918, Eslanda earned her first degree, a B.S. in chemistry from Columbia University.

Upon graduation, her adviser highly recommended her for

a position at Columbia Presbyterian Hospital in New York. The position, as chemist and technician in the Surgical Pathology Department, was traditionally a man's job. In fact, up until that time no black had ever worked at Presbyterian, not even as a porter or a maid. But World War I was at hand and competent personnel were scarce. Eslanda was hired to make microscopic cross-sections of tissues taken from patients in the operating rooms. She describes how her colleagues treated her: "Because I never behaved differently from anyone else, and would not allow anyone to treat me differently, they all came to think of me in some way as not 'Negro,' even though I am obviously Negro in color, hair, and so on. But I did not behave according to their absurd ideas of Negroes, and so they decided that I must be an exception."[89]

In 1920, at an affair in Harlem, she met a "very handsome, but friendly and unspoiled" football player, who was also Phi Beta Kappa.[90] Women all swarmed around him; it was Eslanda's idea to be casual and indifferent, and it worked. Eslanda Goode married Paul Robeson during her first year in medical school; she was twenty-five. Although she continued on with her job at Columbia Presbyterian Hospital for four more years, in 1925 she was forced to quit so that she could travel with her husband to Europe, where they eventually settled—they lived in London for twelve years. Eslanda was very much a part of her husband's career, and she served as his business manager until the birth of their son Paul, Jr., ("Pauli") in 1928.

During this time, Eslanda became interested in photography. She felt that "you have to stay put in a laboratory if you want to work at chemistry" and decided to experiment in a less confining yet personally and scientifically satisfying field.[91] Being a trained scientist, it was plausible that she study photography, and she enrolled in as many courses as she could in London during the late 1920s and early 1930s. Another factor that must have contributed to Eslanda's taking up photography was the fact that photography could uniquely be "her own thing." She had a constant need for self-expansion, yet it had to operate smoothly within her home and personal life. Although she started out taking pictures of her family and friends, she soon set up a darkroom in her home. Her photographic talent was developing by taking pic-

104. Eslanda with Leica camera, 1940

tures every day, and she soon became more than just a competent photographer; she began blending her knowledge in photography with her other work in science and chemistry.

In 1934, she and Paul, along with their friend Mari Seton, traveled to the Soviet Union, where Eslanda took many photographs. In 1935, Eslanda enrolled at the London School of Economics and at London University, where she continued to take photography courses; she also began studying anthropology. In 1936, Eslanda applied for a visa to go to South Africa for anthropological research but was refused. Determined to go, Eslanda decided to take the trip anyway and was accompanied only by her eight-year-old son. She and Pauli boarded a boat and headed for Cape Town without visas. Eslanda had told the South African Embassy in London that she was taking the field trip in conjunction with her anthropological studies at the London School of Economics. She felt that her reason was legitimate but knew that she faced the possibility of not being able to get off the boat when she arrived. So before her departure she telexed ahead to friends in South Africa—Max Yergan and a very well-respected black South African doctor—who were to meet her at the boat. When she and Pauli arrived, they were greeted by Yergan and by the local Africans. Eslanda was granted her visa. The South African government could find no political reason to deny her entrance except that she was Paul Robeson's wife, and Eslanda stuck to her reasons for being in the country. She was able to circulate freely within the intellectual community—doctors, attorneys, scientists—but not with the political community.

The reason why Eslanda was able to move freely in South Africa was that in the 1930s it was truly a police state; there was no chance for disturbance. The country was run like a concentration camp, and the South African people were so closely watched that there was no chance for agitation. Another reason for her independence was that she was a woman scholar, an anthropologist; also, she was traveling with an eight-year-old boy, so she was not considered a threat.

In the earlier days, when she had been Paul's business manager, she was known as a tough negotiator. On this trip she became truly a determined woman. She once stated, "I have never been aggressive and I'm not now. But I have never been meek. I am convinced that meekness invites pushing around, and brings out the worst in people."[92] Yet despite the fact that she was small and rather stocky, she moved with confidence.

Eslanda took pictures wherever she went. In 1949, she went to China, right after the revolution; this time neither Paul nor Pauli could get a passport to go. She left with three American women before the government could get around to restraining her.

The Robesons were great friends with the Carl Van Vechtens. Eslanda and Carl talked a lot about photography. Also in 1939 she met and became friends with photographer Edward Steichen after he made the well-known photograph of Paul as *The Emperor Jones*. Eslanda had a strong bond with the photographic and fine arts communities.

Although she had a Cine-Kodak camera, which her husband had given to her, she also used a Rollex camera. But in the 1940s she used the 35mm Leica, which became her primary camera. Eslanda treated photography as an avocation; it was supplemental to everything else she did in her life. She did, however, shy away from professional editorial criticism. Eslanda was never recognized in the fields of study to which she devoted so much time. Although being the wife of Paul Robeson overshadowed everything she did on her own professionally, her personal satisfaction with her work came from the doing, not from the recognition, and this is evidenced in the legacy she left behind.

105. Jawaharlal Nehru and Indira Gandhi, London, 1938. Essie G. Robeson, photographer

106. China Trip, Mme. Chou En Lai, 1950. Essie G. Robeson, photographer

107. *Fishermens' village, 1946*

108. *Portrait of Eslanda, 1950s*

109. *Eslanda Cardoza Goode,
the photographer's mother*

110. *Paul, Sr., and Jr.*

Elizabeth "Tex" Williams

111. "Tex" on assignment

Elizabeth "Tex" Williams

Elizabeth Williams joined the Women's Army Corps at the age of twenty (her father signed for her) and became an official army photographer. She served in the WACs for twenty-six years and never married; she considered herself "married" to the military. "I could only handle one thing at a time, and I chose military life," she said.

Liz, as she is called by some of her friends (Tex is her other nickname) was born in Houston, Texas, in 1924. Her mother died when she was very young. Liz was raised by her grandmother, who was extremely protective of her. When Liz turned eighteen she wanted to leave home. She thought about joining the WACs but was too young to sign up on her own, and she couldn't get a guardian to sign for her. One day she saw a sign in the window of the Stanley Reddick Art Studio in Houston calling for an assistant. She applied, got the job, and for a year and a half worked for Reddick in his lab; she made appointments, and she also learned the basics of the camera. Subsequently, she bought a Kodak camera and began taking pictures of her friends. This was the beginning of her long association with photography.

Liz wanted to join the service, and she finally convinced her father to sign for her. She said, "Nothing was too difficult for me when I was young. I was brave, confident and adventurous, more adventurous than anything." In 1944, she joined the WACs and was sent to Fort Des Moines in Iowa, an army base for blacks only, where she received her basic training. She did not receive training as a photographer at Fort Des Moines, because there were no photo training courses offered for black WACs. Because of her prior training and experience in the Reddick studio, Liz was sent to Fort Huachuca,

Arizona, where she was assigned to work as a photographer and photo lab technician.

Liz was sent to several other posts across the country while working as a photographer for the Public Information Office; most of her work appeared in local and post newspapers. She was assigned to photograph many different aspects of the army. She did medical photography, photographed army maneuvers, and she shot ID pictures as well as taking defense intelligence photographs. She documented virtually every facet of army life for both the women and the men.

She often went on army air force maneuvers, once flying from Fort Des Moines to Florida to photograph combat maneuvers; she was the only woman on the plane. She took pictures for both air and land combat maneuvers. Some of her photographs show WAC women on the job as nurses or military police, as well as during their free time.

Liz's most difficult assignment was doing medical photography, especially photographing autopsies being conducted. Although she didn't mind having to shoot the adult autopsies, of all her assignments she found having to photograph autopsies of babies the most difficult. This quote reveals her approach to the task: "When you are so military-oriented and you know there is a job to be done, you are going to follow those orders to the end, no matter what it takes to get the job done. You have to be good." She also saw the camera as a mask but, more important, as a tool of human expression. "Sometimes the camera is something you could hide behind in dealing with difficult situations and through the camera you can express yourself and how you feel. Difficulties strengthen the mind just as labor does the body."

In 1949, Liz was sent to the Fort Monmouth, New Jersey, Photo Division School, where she obtained the distinction of being the first black woman to attend and graduate from their photography program. She had been working since 1944 as an official army photographer, but she had never attended the army photo schools because they didn't admit blacks. She graduated first in her class. She went on to work as an intelligence photographer for the defense intelligence agencies, a job that she looked at with disfavor because of the pressure of a possible slip-up in leaking classified information; doing so would mean losing her job. She stayed with the intelligence

Elizabeth "Tex" Williams

112. Listening to the radio at the bamboo fence. Elizabeth "Tex" Williams, U.S. Army Retired, photographer

agencies for four years, was debriefed, and was assigned to teach military correspondence and army administrative subjects at several different army stations. In 1970, Liz retired from the service and moved to Los Angeles. She lived there for two years trying to adjust to civilian life. When she decided the attempt was unsuccessful, she decided to buy a home in Huachuca City, Arizona, not far from Fort Huachuca, where she had been stationed. She still makes her home there.

113. The Photographer

114. "Tex" taking I.D. photos

115. "Tex" making prints in the army lab

116. *WAC nurse, "Enemy Ears Are Listening."*

117. *A WAC-M.P.*

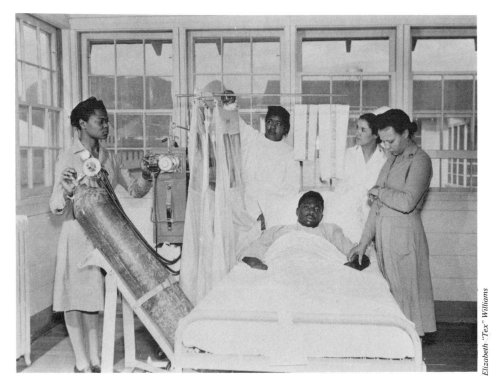

118. WAC nursing staff. Elizabeth "Tex" Williams, U.S. Army Retired, photographer

119. "Tex" among her photo division colleagues

120. *Landscape. Elizabeth "Tex" Williams, U.S. Army Retired, photographer*

Joyce R. Wilson

J oyce Wilson worked as a portrait and fine art photographer in New York City during the 1940s. She moved to California in the 1950s.

121. The Photographer

Ethel Worthington

The Worthington Studio was located in Chicago, on the South Side. It had been a popular, family-operated portrait studio as far back as the 1920s. Ethel Worthington was an assistant to her husband for many years, but after his death in the 1940s, she continued running the photography studio, doing mostly portrait work.

122. Worthington Studios

Part 4

HISTORICAL OVERVIEW

1950–1970

The black population in major American cities like Detroit, Chicago, New York, and Philadelphia was on a steady increase during the years between 1950 and 1960. In fact, over one and a half million blacks migrated from the South to Northern and Western regions between 1950 and 1960. California, Illinois, and New York were the most popular states in which to relocate. Slowly, the government was becoming more sensitive to the unfair and unequal treatment of blacks across the country. The Supreme Court was frequently faced with cases dealing with racial segregation. Black men and women were becoming more of a part of the mainstream in American society. Figures show that the income of black families increased during World War II; this was primarily due to the migration and the higher wages paid in the larger urban areas. The median family income for nonwhite families increased from $2,700 in 1947 to $3,300 in 1962.[93]

In 1950, the U. S. Census counted 52,890 photographers of both sexes: 8,550 were women.[94] The total number of black women who listed themselves as photographers was 240. Of that number, only 180 of them were employed.[95]

According to the 1950 census, the median age of all women photographers was 34.6 years, and over one-half of them were married. The median income for all female photographers in 1950 was $1,500 a year. In a book published by the U. S. Department of Labor's Women's Bureau in 1954, entitled *Negro Women and Their Jobs*, the point is made that black women were finding more employment in the professional and technical category.[96] Although photographers were listed in this category, most of the 105,000 black women listed in technical categories were teachers. The 1954 Census of Business listed over 17,000 photographic studios operating, but there was no breakdown for women photographers. The combined total revenue for these studios was $334,055 a year.[97]

The 1950s were years of achievement for black women. But although Gwendolyn Brooks was awarded a Pulitzer Prize for poetry in Chicago and Edith Sampson was appointed an alternate delegate to the United Nations, Rosa Parks was ordered to give up her seat to a white man on a bus in Montgomery, Alabama. Her refusal touched off an organized protest that eventually led to the Supreme Court decision declaring segregation on public transportation unconstitutional. *The Pittsburgh Courier* ran an article on January 27, 1951, praising the achievements of black women in "arts and professions."[98] Black business registers published in the big cities showed and cited advertisements for black women's photography studios. The Louise Martin Art Studio, for example, a photographic studio in Houston, was doing a good business.

In 1955, an important photographic exhibition, *The Family of Man*, was held at the Museum of Modern Art in New York. Edward Steichen, thought of by many as the dean of American photographers and who was the director of the department of photography at the Museum of Modern Art, was the principal organizer. In the exhibition and in the exhibition's book, Steichen chose not only photographs of family life the world over but also photographs that were metaphors for life and that were the work of both black and white, male and female photographers.

Steichen was cited by the National Urban League "for making mankind proud of its humanity,"[99] and the Urban League's executive director, Edward S. Lewis, during a citation ceremony at the museum, described *The Family of Man* as one of "the great poems of our time, taking us on an odyssey through all the myriad of human experience." The Urban League's citation to Steichen read: "Seeking equality of opportunity for negroes with all Americans, the Urban League works for the benefit of all peoples, building toward the creation of a true Family of Man. Edward Steichen's exhibition narrates the Urban League's credo with an eloquence seldom before seen or heard."[100] This was a monumental step toward bridging the wide gap between black and white America, but it was also proof, positive proof, that the art of photography could communicate understanding, compassion, and feelings to mankind during a time of chaotic divisiveness in America. Photography had a quiet yet monumental impact; it reached out during a time of turbulence in the country, at a time when the white photography world was finally willing to allow the power of the medium to make an important statement.

Nineteen fifty-four was an important year for civil rights; the Supreme Court declared in Brown *vs.* The Board of Education that "separate but equal" educational facilities were "inherently unequal." Segregation was declared unconstitutional.[101] Following this decision, about 150 previously segregated schools became integrated.

In 1964, the Office of Economic Opportunity (OEO) was formed. One of its projects was to hire a team of photographers, who were assigned to photograph people aided by government programs and the progress that was being made as a result of government programs designed to combat poverty. The basis of the photographic work of the OEO was very similar to that of the Farm Security Administration (FSA) of the 1930s. Even the images were strikingly similar, but so were the rules and requirements for being a staff photographer. As with the FSA, there were no black women photographers hired by the OEO.

Black women photographers were finding jobs with black programs and organizations. Phillda Ragland-Njau, who was employed by the United Presbyterian Church, was responsible for photographing social and economic projects that the church sponsored in different countries around the world. Elaine Tomlin, known for her images of urban riots, rural poverty, and civil rights marchers, went on to become the official photographer for the Southern Christian Leadership Conference. In addition to the civil rights marches, photographer Mikki Ferrill covered street gang activity on Chicago's South Side.

The number of blacks migrating from the South to the Northern cities dropped during the 1960s. Blacks were overcrowded in the cities where they had settled. Black women were 13.1 percent of the labor force.[102] The 1960 census indicated a total of 52,171 photographers, a slight decrease from the previous decade, and 143 black women photographers, a decrease from 1950.[103] Also, the median age for female photographers was slightly older than it had been in 1950. The median income for female photographers on the whole was $2,628 a year. The Census of Business in 1963 counted 19,544 photographic studios, a decrease from the 20,026 studios counted in 1958.[104] As a result, the income in these studios increased in 1963, although the actual number of establishments decreased.

In 1963, President Kennedy declared segregation "morally wrong." But less than ten percent of black public school students were in integrated classes. It was during that year that Medgar Evers and John Kennedy were assassinated and violence swept through the nation. The mid-1960s saw scores of riots and demonstrations across the country.

Violence heightened in 1968 when Dr. Martin Luther King, Jr., was assassinated. In more than a hundred cities, there was looting, shooting, and burning, and thousands of people were hurt and arrested. Black photographers also became targets of violence in their attempts to document the struggles, as seen in a front page story of *The New York Times* from 1965 entitled "Klansman Is Arrested After Attack on Negro Cameraman in Georgia."

The civil rights movement had begun in the Deep South during the mid-1950s and lasted for about fifteen years. The climax came in 1968, when black and white Americans mourned the assassination of Dr. King. Louise Martin was one of several photographers who covered the famous leader's funeral, contributing to the important documentation of that event.

Mikki Ferrill

Valeria "Mikki" Ferrill was born in Chicago, on May 12, 1937. Her early upbringing did not allow for many idle moments. She took violin and ballet lessons and attended Saturday morning classical concerts. Her mother refused to buy a television because it demanded too much of Mikki's attention. So at an early age, Mikki was exposed to a variety of art forms. She remembers studying photographs in books and magazines as a child. But by the time she began photographing, she had already experienced several art forms, such as drawing, sculpture, and jewelry making. Mikki attended the Art Institute in Chicago, majoring in design. At the same time she was involved in making jewelry. Mikki said, "I was still searching for that perfect medium to pursue my artistic expression." Then she met Chicago photographer Ted Williams and discovered photography as an art form. It immediately became her visual medium. She says, "It was upon viewing his work that I really changed my perspective of photography. Up until that time I looked upon photography as a means of recording the times and news. Not until seeing Ted's work did I realize what a tremendous art form photography was. I finished that semester at the Art Institute and enrolled in a class Ted was offering."

The photography class taught by Williams consisted of thirteen students. Among its members were Roy Lewis, Bill Grant, Chester Sheard, and several other accomplished photographers. Mikki was the only woman and the only beginner in the class. In 1967, after completing Williams's class, Mikki moved to Mexico, where she worked as a freelance foreign correspondent, and took on several assignments for the *Mexico This Month* publication.

After returning to the United States in 1970, Mikki felt confident that her technique was intact. It was also apparent to her that she had developed a personal style. Mikki has been dedicated to photography and has been shooting for over twenty years, and her achievements have been many. Her credits include published work in magazines such as *Time, Ebony,* and *Jet,* and in newspapers such as *The Chicago Tribune* and the *Chicago Defender.* Mikki's photographic work has also been widely exhibited, including at the Sheppared Gallery in Chicago; the South Side Community Art Center in Chicago; Lincoln Center in New York City; the Museum of Modern Art in San Francisco; and the Black Photographers' Annual Traveling Exhibition in the USSR.

Mikki comments on her relationship with photography: "Photography was the medium that could give me all the aspects I wanted in an art form: the ability to record the situation as it truly appeared yet with a personal interpretation. But more importantly, photography involves the total spectrum from reality to total abstract. There are many techniques that enhance one's artistic endeavors. The range of photography is so vast that the involvement can be all consuming." Obviously, this photographer's love affair with photography will continue for a long time to come.

123. Graffiti, Chicago street gangs

© Mikki Ferrill/Photography

124. Dr. King

© Mikki Ferrill/Photography

125. Dr. King at the Freedom Festival

Inge Hardison

126. *The Photographer*

Inge Hardison

A native of Portsmouth, Virginia, Inge Hardison attended the Art Students' League in New York City, where she studied painting, sculpture, and photography. During the 1950s, Inge worked as an actress, artist's model, and teacher. At the same time she worked as a freelance photographer selling her stories and pictures to various publications. Her work was frequently seen in *Color* magazine in the early 1950s. Most of her work has been in portraiture, with children being her favorite subject. Hardison is a founding member of the Black Academy of Arts and Letters. She is currently continuing her successful work in sculpture and has completed a series of historical portraits of black leaders in cast stone.

Inge Hardison now resides in New York City.

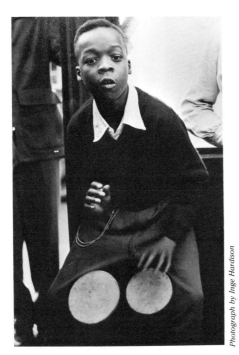

Photograph by Inge Hardison

127. *Bongo player*

Photograph by Inge Hardison

128. *Young man with cowbell*

Photograph by Inge Hardison

129. *Street music*

Master Sergeant Grendel A. Howard

WAC professional photographer M. Sgt. Grendel A. Howard is here pictured shortly before a tour of duty that took her to Vietnam in 1968. She went into the army with a background in advertising and marketing. Selected many times as "Outstanding WAC" during her first assignment as editor of her installation newspaper, she quit the army for three years to continue her college studies.

After Vietnam, where she was awarded the Bronze Star, Howard returned to the States and adopted a three-year-old boy, making her one of the first single WACs to adopt a child. From 1974 to 1976 she worked in the TRADOC Public Affairs Office at Fort Monroe, in Hampton, Virginia.

U.S. Army Photo

130. The Photographer

Louise Jefferson

orn in Washington, D.C., Louise Jefferson knew at an early age that she wanted to pursue a career in either music or art. The art influence came from her father, whose occupation included engraving bank charters and other formal documents for the U. S. Treasury. Louise's interest in music came from her mother, who was an accomplished musician. Louise attended Hunter College before she began a twenty-six-year career with a New York publishing firm. She worked from 1942 to 1960 as art director and production assistant for Friendship Press, the publishing arm of the National Council of Churches. She has also done art and photographic work for many of the major publishing houses in New York: Doubleday, Viking, the Rutgers University Press, Bookcraftsmen Associates. She designed the African American Institute's logo. Her freelance career has seen her illustrating hundreds of books and selling innumerable photographs to book publishers. "I couldn't eat without my camera. I don't go to the wood pile without it," she says.

The Decorative Arts of Africa, which was researched, written, and illustrated with drawings and photographs acquired during five trips to Africa over a ten-year period, is perhaps one of the best known of Jefferson's works and is one of her proudest accomplishments. She obtained two Ford Foundation Fellowships to finance the trips. Only about a third of the materials she gathered were used in the book.

Louise taught metalwork and painting in the studio workshop of the late Augusta Savage, one of the important figures of the Harlem Renaissance. She is a member of the American Institute of Graphic Arts, the Photographic Society of America, Alpha Kappa Alpha sorority, and the executive commit-

Louise E. Jefferson

131. Louis Armstrong

Louise E. Jefferson

132. Autumn fog

tee of the Women's Africa Committee, and is also a consultant for the Gallery of Modern Art in New York. Her works have been exhibited at the Baltimore Museum of Art, the African American Institute, the Schomburg Center for Research in Black Culture, the New York Public Library, and the New York Bank for Savings. Her awards include a U. S. Government Commission Certificate of Recognition for Outstanding Achievement, their Certificate of Special Merit (1957 and 1960), and a Ford Foundation Fellowship Special Award.

Jefferson lives in Litchfield, Connecticut, and is still an active photographer.

Louise E. Jefferson

133. Alabama boy

Louise Martin

134. The Photographer

Louise Martin

ouise Martin always knew what she wanted to be. The fact that her father was a waiter and her mother a maid helped her to make her decision that she was going to be a professional at something. She was born January 9, 1914, in Brenham, Texas, a small German community not far from Houston.

She was intrigued by pictures during her childhood. When she was eleven, her mother bought her a Kodak box camera. "There was an old German that operated a studio at my hometown," Louise says. "My mother bought the camera from him and he would do the processing. I fell in love with it as a child. Taking pictures was my greatest fun."[105]

As a schoolgirl, Louise snapped pictures of her family and friends. Around 1930, she moved to Houston. She became her high school's photographer. Determined to become a professional, Louise looked at college seriously and aimed for a degree in photography. She worked as a domestic to pay her way through school. "Being a maid, that's an honorable profession, but that's not what I want to do the rest of my life. I wanted one person in my family to be a success,"[106] she says. "My mother would have sent me to Prairie View College [a black Texas school] as it was very close to us and the rates were relatively reasonable, but what Prairie View offered, I did not want. Home economics and nursing and that sort of thing. I always wanted to be a photographer and pursue my art."[107] No white schools in the South were open to her, so Louise left Texas and went to Chicago to study at the Art Institute and at the American School of Photography. Louise soon left Chicago and entered Denver University in Colorado, where she eventually earned her degree in photography from the university's School of Photographic Arts and Sciences. She was the only black woman enrolled in the school at that time.

Louise's determination and drive pushed her to put forth every effort to be really good at whatever she did, and that was photography. It was her first love and her only one. She was confident of her talent and wanted to make a living from it.

The World War II years gave Louise a real opportunity. "That was a time when a photographer who really knew his business could have gotten rich, because soldiers were constantly having pictures made to send back home to their girlfriends and families. Anytime there is a war, there are two things you can count on—a lot of babies and a lot of picture making." Louise knew other photographers while she was at Denver University who opened photo studios near the army camps and who did quite well. Soldiers even came to the university photo school to have their pictures made. She remembers, "People didn't have a lot of cameras of their own, like now, and a professional photographer could really make it. Now, every third person you meet has a camera. It doesn't always mean he knows how to use it but he has one." Around 1945, Louise got married, but the marriage was a brief one. "I wanted to follow my talent, and he played no role in my success,"[108] she says. Although she married a "traditional" man, Louise was unwilling to lead a traditional life staying home to be a housewife. Her husband wanted her to choose between marriage and her photography career. He was not willing to allow her to do both. She chose her career.

In 1946, at the age of thirty-two, Louise became the owner and operator of a portrait and commercial studio that she established in Houston. When she decided to open the studio, she had to get several people to write letters proving that she was serious about going into business. "If I had been in the service I would have been one of the first to get a camera, but you just couldn't get them, and then it would be on order six months before you can get it. Many plants had to stop making cameras because so many of the supplies were being used for wartime purposes."

Despite setbacks, Louise's spirits were never dampened, and the Louise Martin Art Studio finally served Houston's

Louise Martin

135. *Louise Martin's business card*

Photograph by Louise Martin

136. Street scene in Tulsa

black community—schools and churches—as well as the social world. She became known as Houston's "society photographer."[109] In addition to having started her own business, Louise also bought her own home in 1955, which she paid off in twelve years.

She was the only black photographer, male or female, to become a member of the Southwestern Photographers Convention. As a member of the Rocky Mountain Association, Louise attended its annual convention in the early 1950s. The president of the organization asked Louise to join the Southwestern Photographers Convention and to exhibit five of her photographs, which would be hung alongside the works of the other members, all of whom were white. At first Louise declined the offer on the grounds that the hotel where the convention and exhibition took place did not allow blacks to ride in its elevators. The president arranged to have the exhibition hung in the hotel's mezzanine. Louise would not have to use the elevator. She joined the organization and became its first black member. Of the exhibition, Louise says, "You didn't know a black photographer from a white because you were not allowed to put your name on your work, plus the fact that there were a lot of white photographers who had photographed little black children. The whites got a kick out of photographing cute little black kids or an old black lady with a corn pipe in her mouth." Since she was a member, nobody knew who Louise Martin was, but she was the only member who was selected to exhibit every photo that she entered. And since everyone's curiosity was aroused, the president introduced Louise to the members at the opening of the exhibit. Louise remembers: "They all came over to me with the biggest hugs and handshakes that you ever saw in your life. It was 1952, and the beginning of my association with the Texas Professional Photographers." She joined the Professional Photographers of America, Texas Professional Photographers Association, Southwestern Professional Photographers of Texas, and the Business and Professional Women's Association.

Louise's approach to the photographic business is revealed in a simple question. "How could the cosmetic companies sell their product if they didn't have their pretty colored brochures?" she asked. "There's nothing in the world you can do without photography. You couldn't even get a job digging a ditch without an application and you must have a photograph on that." Louise was confident of her work and knew the market. She knew she could make money off of women because, as she says, "I made them look good."

Louise always felt that part of the secret of being successful was looking the part. She loved driving fancy cars and liked "good clothes." She worked hard to get them. In 1967, Louise was presented the Outstanding Business Woman of the Year Award by the Houston League of Business and Professional Women. In 1968, she was one of the national press cadre in Atlanta, Georgia, providing photo news coverage of the funeral of Dr. Martin Luther King, Jr. Louise covered the funeral for *The Forward Times* and *The Informer*, two black Houston newspapers. It was an experience she says she will never forget. "People stayed up all night [before the funeral], nobody slept. Hotels even gave away free rooms. They just gave the city over to the blacks."[110] Louise had been a great admirer of Dr. King and once had had the opportunity to photograph him in Houston when he spoke at the graduation ceremony of a local black business college.

Louise was cited by *The Houston Chronicle* at a ceremony in 1969 that honored black women in the community.[111] By the early 1970s, she had received twenty-seven awards in photography. She became so well known in Houston's black community that she was often called on to give professional advice. In 1973, she founded the Louise Martin School of Photography, offering courses in all branches of photography. Her "complete photo course" consisted of sixteen weeks in training, two hours a day, four days a week. She offered an intensive study of each aspect of black and white photography. Her school also offered à la carte courses such as Fundamental Photography, Advanced Techniques, Flash Photography, Advanced Portraiture, Commercial and Industrial Techniques, and Photo Oil Coloring. Louise's school was located in the heart of Houston, and she even enrolled out-of-town students. Her school operated for about three years and then ran into financial difficulties. It closed in 1976.

Louise didn't give up, she continued with her freelance work. Now in her seventies, she has no intention of retiring. A determined teacher and craftsperson, Louise feels that she

Photograph by Louise Martin

137. Dr. Martin L. King, Jr.

Photograph by Louise Martin

*138. Dr. King, speaking at a college commencement,
being congratulated by the college president*

Photograph by Louise Martin

139. The King family being escorted at funeral

140. A young Jesse Jackson at Dr. King's funeral

141. The King family at Martin Luther King, Jr.'s funeral

has led an interesting life. "I want to leave something here in hopes that some child would see my work and learn of my life and be encouraged to do the same thing." As a photographer she has both survived and made a living. "It was my living, and when, you know, you got to make a living, take care of your expenses and obligations, it means that you must work. So I think that was chiefly how I felt aside from my love for the work," she says. "I didn't get rich, but I made a good living."

Photograph by Louise Martin

142. A portrait

Photograph by Louise Martin

143. A portrait

Phillda Ragland-Njau

Phillda Ragland-Njau, born in Plainfield, New Jersey, in 1939, was the first black woman photographer to be sent on overseas mission assignments by the United Presbyterian Church. At twenty-nine, Phillda was the manager of production for the filmstrip and photography section of the Commission on Ecumenical Missions and Relations—the Overseas Department of the United Presbyterian Church in the United States. Phillda comments, "Being the first black woman photographer in the church of course made a difference, but I thought of my assignment more as a personal journey into life, self-development, self-discovery, and opportunity for spiritual growth through involvement with people." She goes on to say, "It is the aesthetic and spiritual dimension of photography that interests me, and which I try to put across in my work whether I am photographing a person, a natural thing, or an object."

Her assignments occurred during the height of the civil rights movement, and in 1969 Phillda was the subject of a photo feature in *Ebony* magazine. Phillda's responsibilities abroad included photographing the social and economic projects that the church sponsors in many foreign countries. Some of her most interesting photographs were collected for an exhibition, "Kids Next Door," that drew large crowds to the church's headquarters in New York. Many of her photos have been published in church-oriented publications as well as in *Ebony*, *Jet*, and *Popular Photography*. At the same time that she was teaching an adult education class in scriptwriting and in shooting and editing motion pictures, Phillda received her Master's degree at Columbia University.

Phillda Ragland-Njau

144. *African woman and child*

Initially hired as a photo librarian for the United Presbyterian Church, Phillda's big break came when Fred Haines, photographer for the home office, taught her the basic camera techniques. "Fred was patient and most helpful," Phillda says, "He gave up weekends to guide me along. He gave me my first and only lessons in photography and then bowed out to see me on my way."[112] When her boss, Dr. Archie Crouch, noticed her progress, he sent her to Latin America for her first overseas assignment. This was a boost to Phillda's confidence. On her assignment to South America, she used an old Rollei-cord 120 box camera and a separate hand meter. She credited that camera with the capacity to take excellent photographs but realized later, after graduating to the 35mm camera, just how bulky and awkward the box camera was. Phillda was later called to do several other short-term assignments, including conferences and photo features for articles about black women. As the official photographer for a black clergymen's conference in St. Louis, she was among the handful of women in the assembly of about four hundred black clergymen. She was the only woman photographer, however; the other press members were males. In 1970, the state of New Jersey named her one of its Outstanding Young Women of America.

It was on her last overseas assignment to East Africa that she met her husband, Elimo Njau, an East African mural painter. He invited her to join the East African International Arts Program, which sponsored two art centers, one in Tanzania and the other, PaaYaPaa Art Gallery, in Nairobi, Kenya. Phillda credits photography with turning her toward a new direction in her life. She has been in East Africa for over ten years now and since 1974 has been working exclusively with the overall program of the Kibo Art Gallery in Tanzania which is situated at the bottom of Africa's highest mountain, Kilimanjaro.

Phillda's most recent photographs can be seen in *The Daily Nation*, a daily Nairobi newspaper for which she does freelance work. Ultimately, she would like to do picture books for children.

145. South American girl. Phillda Ragland, photographer

146. South American child. Phillda Ragland, photographer 147. Taking a break. Phillda Ragland, photographer

148. Learning to read. Phillda Ragland, photographer

Adine Williams

149. The Photographer

Adine Williams

Anative of Louisiana, Adine Williams, then Adine Mitchell, began photographing in 1936 when she took a job in The Wiltz Photography Studio in New Orleans. Adine was in high school at the time and credits Wiltz with teaching her the basics of photography.

In the 1940s, Adine married a photographer, and together they opened the McLain Studio in New Orleans. Business was good at the McLain Studio during the war. Their studio was across the street from a USO Center, and Adine had to hire four people to help operate the business.

Later, Adine and her husband divorced. She became the proprietor of her own studio, Camera Masters, in New Orleans, and she remarried. Adine and Eddie Williams conducted a successful photography studio in New Orleans but soon decided to move their business to California, where they set up Camera Masters in Monterey. After enjoying many successful years in California, Adine and Eddie moved back to Louisiana, where they are currently owners and operators of another studio, the Picture Place, in Baton Rouge.

Along with her successful portrait work, Adine did many of the class photos for Dillard and Xavier universities in New Orleans. She also found time during her career to mother three children—two boys and one girl—who have all gone on to be professional photographers. (See Leah Ann Washington in Part 5.)

It has been a pleasure to work with all of you at Dillard University.

Through the eyes of these cameras over 30,000 individuals have been recorded, including babies, children, communions, weddings, family groups, and organizations.

Work of whatever nature is to render service, in obedience to God's law. God bless each and every one of you.

Camera Masters Studio
EDDIE & ADINE WILLIAMS

Adine Williams

150. A Dillard University yearbook advertisement

Adine Williams

151. Camera Masters Studio, 1946–1956

Part 5

HISTORICAL

OVERVIEW

1970–1985

At the beginning of the 1970s, the stated theme for black artists and craftsmen was black awareness. This was evidenced and echoed in the photographs of black women photographers like Mikki Ferrill and Elaine Tomlin. The reportage done by these and other women brought the world closer to an understanding of what took place during the civil rights struggle.

The black civilian labor force continued to expand at a rapid pace in 1970 despite the lack of available jobs.[113] This was a direct result of the civil rights movement of the 1960s, which advocated and strengthened fair employment programs. There was a great deal of pressure brought to bear on American businesses for equal opportunity and job training for the black workforce. This pressure was seen even as far away as South Africa, and in 1971 black employees of Polaroid put pressure on the company to withdraw from South Africa in protest of that country's policy of racial separation. As a result, Polaroid sponsored a project to counteract apartheid in South Africa "from within the system" with an experiment to improve the wages of nonwhite workers and by providing opportunities for advanced job training.[114] This alternative to the company's withdrawal from the country, which was what American black employees had demanded, proved to be constructive for a period of years, and it even drew praise from some black South African leaders. Gatsha Buthelethzi, chief of the Zulu tribe, urged Polaroid not to withdraw but rather to earnestly attempt to improve conditions. He applauded Polaroid's efforts, saying, "Any change in the day to day life of a black man in this country is something very essential."[115]

In 1970, the U. S. Census Bureau released statistics on photographers based on a "sample" listing, counting only a small percentage. The most startling evidence presented by the figures was the wide gap between the income of male and female photographers. The American male photographer's median income was more than twice that of the female photographer. The median age for female photographers was 38.5 years; black female photographers were older than their white female counterparts by ten years.[116]

It was not until the early 1970s that photography gained public acceptance as an art form. The efforts of some major museums to provoke interest in photography as an art, such as Steichen's 1955 *Family of Man* exhibition at the Museum of Modern Art, influenced museums across the country, and they began collecting, buying, and exhibiting photographs. Collecting photographs became a trend. Auction houses like Sotheby Parke Bernet and Christie's, both in New York and London, held their first photography auctions. Soon galleries and museums in Europe and the United States sought photographs to provide for the now photography-conscious public. For much of the 1970s, photography was not only an accepted art form; it also quickly became an investment, in much the same way that other collectible art forms like painting and sculpture were considered good barriers against inflation. As a result, these new collectors, young and affluent professionals and business executives, pushed the art of photography into elitism.

Meanwhile, the photography experts, talking only to one another, had little dialogue with those outside their circles. In a 1971 *New York Times* article, photography critic A. D. Coleman attacked this elitist approach to photography, saying, "Photography is so thoroughly interwoven into the fabric of our culture that the warp of our culture and the loom of history are absolutely depended upon it for stability."[117] In his article, Coleman noted similarities in thinking between the military and the photography experts: each divided the population into two groups. For the military, the division was between soldiers and civilians; in photography, the division was between "serious" photographers as opposed to amateurs and nonphotographers.[118] Coleman felt that the formation of cliques would be a great disadvantage to the general public, who were all affected in some way by the photographic image. He suggested that the photography experts spread their knowledge throughout the culture, stressing photography's great advantage as a common communicator. A new generation of people had grown up in front of a television set; they were also accustomed to picture magazines like *Life, Look*, and *National Geographic*. Almost everything the 1970s generation encountered—from advertisements to family and world events—was communicated through photography.

For this reason, Coleman urged that everyone "in the larger photographic community" be educated in the functions of the photographic image.[119] As a culture, we were receiving as much information from the photographic image as we were from the written word, and possibly fifty percent of our decisions were in some way based on visual input. To exclude the public, which is so affected by the everyday use of photographs, from the knowledge of the photography community, did, indeed, pose a great threat.

What was happening in the 1970s was the newfound awareness of photography's ability to allow us to look at ourselves, our relatives, and our friends at different times in our lives through family albums and also to view ourselves and sense our time and place in the world. For black Americans this vision of past and present was of extreme importance, and much of the vision was communicated through photography.

Although black photographers were excluded from photographic history, images of blacks were not. Photography critic Jonathan Green, in his 1984 book, *American Photography: A Critical History 1945 to the Present*, commented on photographs of blacks through the work of white photographer Robert Frank. Green wrote: "There is more human intensity, joy, meditation, and grief in the photographs of blacks than in the photographs of whites. There is more feeling emanating from the omni-present juke box than from the entertainments of high culture."[120]

Green stated that "American democratic culture is hostile to anything that smacks of special treatment." He said, "Art should be the expression of the masses, not the expression of the few . . . and, in fact photography has become the most democratic of all arts."[121] At the same time, he did not include one black photographer in his entire book, a book that spans a significantly active period for black photographers, 1945 to

1984. Does "special treatment" not refer to elitism? Even the 1982 edition of Beaumont Newhall's *The History of Photography*, a standard text, did not mention one black photographer.[122] These omissions, one cannot help but conclude, must be intentional, because the black contribution to American photography has been substantial. If the photography experts continue to tout the notion of "democracy," for which photography no doubt has the potential, in the light of white America's elitist attitude, then the very words "democratic art" will be a travesty.

Kamoinge Workshop, a black photographers' organization, was formed by black Guggenheim fellowship recipient (1955) Roy DeCarava in the early 1970s out of a need to communicate and share the photographic dialogue flowing throughout the black community, a dialogue that was not being heard by the elitist whites in the profession. Black photographers' needs more than justified Kamoinge. Kamoinge constituted a means for them to share their ideas with one another and to exhibit work that contained sensitive images of black life in America.

A new book, *The Black Photographer's Annual*, showcased the work of many black photographers, both male and female. Its first edition was published in 1973; the second in 1974; the third in 1978; and the fourth in 1980.[123] Because of financial difficulties, publication ceased after 1980. But many black photographers' work was seen there for the first time. Some of the women photographers featured in *The Annual* were Elaine Tomlin, Mikki Ferrill, Cary Beth Cryor, and Ming Smith, all different in style, but strong in their ability to communicate thoughts, forms, and ideas through photography. No pioneer women like Vera Jackson and Louise Martin were ever featured in the book, although several of the pioneer men, such as P. H. Polk, James Van Der Zee, Roy DeCarava, and Gordon Parks, all had portfolios published in different editions.

Life magazine, an elite publication of the establishment, invented what became known as "the star system." *Life* seemed to hire only certain photographers and always the same ones. They created a situation in which the event being covered came to be less important than the photographer covering it.[124] Although other picture publications tried to set up a similar situation, *Life* especially encouraged this star system.[125]

This system had a bad rippling effect: as a result of it, young photographers were compelled to become famous as early in their careers as possible. They were trapped into repeating their earlier successes and were rendered afraid to explore new and uncharted potentials of the craft. Because of the great new boom of young white photographers, competition became so keen that it made job opportunities scarce and almost impossible for the black photographer. Only a few made it, and even fewer survived. Those who did survive carried on the elitist tradition. With the demise of *Life* in the early 1970s, new standards were free to develop, since the criteria for judging photographs had been so strongly dictated by that one picture magazine.

Meanwhile, the boom in the photography market continued in the United States, prices soared, and collectors continued to buy photographs. Some dealers were even shifting their attention from paintings to photographs, and one New York City art dealer boasted of sales of photographic prints totaling nearly $750,000.[126] Next on the horizon was the arrival of a new crop of celebrity photographers. The national press enjoyed covering Susan Ford, daughter of former President Gerald Ford, when she applied for a position on the photography staff of *The Washington Post*.[127] Her admittance to a photography school made front pages. Caroline Kennedy, daughter of former President John F. Kennedy, made news when she joined the staff of ABC for a brief stint as a photographer.[128] And then there was Margaret Trudeau, who used photography to inform the world of her independence.[129]

Black magazines like *Ebony, Essence, Encore,* and *Black Enterprise* have showcased the work of some black women photographers. Jo Moore Stewart, Rosetta Teasdale, Barbara DuMetz, Lydia Hammond, and Gwen Phillips were all cited as accomplished photographers. *Essence* magazine noted that Leah Ann Washington was the first black woman graduate of the Brooks Institute of Photography in California.[130] Leah's interest in photography grew out of her family's photography business, which was started by her mother, Adine Williams, in New Orleans around 1937.

By the end of the 1970s, a whole new crop of photographers had arrived. For black photographers, much of this coming of age was aided by black publications and the need for companies to comply with equal opportunity employment laws. Black women benefited from the latter; they fulfilled dual requirements—they were women and they were black. But even when *Life* magazine made a second go of it at the end of the 1970s, its editors still had not assigned work to one black woman photographer and the work of only a few black men had been published.

The 1980 U. S. Census reported 72,496 male and 22,266 female photographers. Of that number, 840 were black women.[131] Photography and history of photography courses were on the rise in colleges and universities across the country. Thirty-eight U. S. universities offered Master of Fine Arts degrees in photography.[132] As universities began to recognize photography, so did many art publications, such as *Art News, Art in America, Art Forum*, and *The Village Voice*; all ran pieces about photography. While few early photographers had university degrees, now the university was their tie to the art world.

Today, black women photographers are working at jobs that were traditionally reserved for men and whites. Ruby Washington is a staff photographer for *The New York Times*. Michelle Agins, an ambitious photographer who lives in Chicago, landed a position as the official photographer to the mayor of Chicago. In Washington, D.C., Julia Jones was the personal photographer to the Reverend Jesse Jackson on his trip to Syria to free American soldier Robert Goodman.

And finally, the long-awaited traveling exhibition, curated by Valencia Hollins Coar, a black woman scholar, placed the black photographer formally into the history of photography. The exhibit, *A Century of Black Photographers*, clearly showed the many years of black involvement in photography. In "A Century of Black Photographers," *New York Times* writer C. Gerald Fraser reviewed the seven-city touring exhibition, mentioning the only black woman photographer included, and that was Elise Harleston, whose first name was stated mistakenly as Eva.[133] There were no photographs taken by women featured in the exhibition, even though it spanned over a hundred years and was curated by a woman. Fraser stated that "historically most black women photographers worked in anonymity with their husbands."[134] While this was partially true, the careers of Mary Flenoy, Mary Warren, and Jennie Welcome contradict that theory.

Employment for photographers is expected to grow more slowly than the average for all occupations through the mid-1990s, according to the Census Bureau.[135] In some areas demand will be stimulated as business and industry place greater emphasis upon visual aids and presentations and on public relations work. Employment in photojournalism is expected to continue to grow slowly. Competition for jobs in all areas of photography is expected to remain keen.

What black women photographers can expect for the future can only depend on how hard they are willing to work. As history has demonstrated, success in the field of photography requires three times the effort of that in any field. But the persistence and perseverance of black women, proven throughout the last one hundred years, says that it can be done. It is key to remember that photography is only fifty years younger than the United States. And while it has continued to play a key role in the shaping of our self-image as women, we must remain vigilant, we must continue to contribute our thoughts, ideas, and images as black American women photographers if we are to be truly integrated into the fabric of and remain contributors to American history.

Michelle Agins

She states her goal as "reporting and recording life as it happens so that future generations will have a pictorial history of the past." Since the seventh grade, Michelle Agins, a native of Chicago, was the only girl in her school photography club. She took pictures for the school paper with an old Brownie box camera, which she took from the shelf of her grandmother's house, and developed her film by using a pan, "just like laundry."

At thirty years of age, Michelle is still the only woman in her photography club, but she now shoots with Nikons and

152. Michelle V. Agins in front of City Hall. Bob Black, photographer

her club and darkroom are in the Chicago City Hall. She is the official photographer to Mayor Harold Washington and takes his picture whenever and wherever he goes. Her job demands that she be at his side constantly: during press conferences, when he greets important visitors, at banquets, rallies, speeches, and through the long hours of City Council debates. In addition to shooting both candid and posed photos, Michelle is responsible for developing and editing her own work as she matches her photographs to the press releases that flow each day from City Hall to Chicago's newspapers.

Each night, Michelle must review the mayor's schedule for the following day, planning photo opportunities with press secretary Grayson Mitchell, to whom she is electronically tethered by a tiny signal beeper. Michelle also runs occasional interference for Mayor Washington when he is waylaid by television reporters eager for a spontaneous quote. She spends the rest of her time standing at the back of the City Council chamber, "watching, listening, and learning."

In 1968, while Michelle was taking pictures near the apartment building that her grandparents managed on Chicago's South Side, she noticed a man watching her. He asked her, "Do you know what you're doing?" When she replied, "Sure," he handed her a 35mm camera and said, "Here, shoot with this." The man turned out to be *Chicago Daily News* photographer John Tweedle, and this chance encounter would affect Michelle's life forever. John Tweedle and his wife virtually adopted Michelle, whose parents, a marine and a nurse, were both dead by the time she was eight. Soon Michelle was dividing her time between the Tweedles' comfortable home and the apartment she shared with her grandparents in a neighborhood where junkies and gang wars were common. A close relationship grew and lasted until Tweedle's sudden death in 1981.

"Although he said he was going to make me the best photographer in the world, Tweedle really wanted me to be a doctor," Michelle recalls. She entered Loyola University as a premed student but realized after a year "that I was a photographer. Journalism was in my blood. I was doomed." So she got a part-time job as a copy girl and preschool sports photographer at the old *Chicago Daily News*.

On the recommendation of a magazine editor, Michelle

landed a job with *Encore* magazine in New York, where for a year she took pictures of performers, while also freelancing for *The New York Times, Newsweek*, and several women's magazines. But she grew homesick for her family and decided to return to Chicago in 1974, intent on finishing college. She entered Rosary College, where she majored in communication arts and sciences. She took a semester of independent study in London, photographing and interviewing people throughout the London parks. She paid for these studies with her earnings from magazine assignments. Michelle decided at graduation that she wanted to be the President's official photographer. She applied directly to the White House, but didn't get an answer.

Reasoning that the mayor of Chicago needed the same service, Michelle approached an alderman for advice. He sent her to the city's Department of Human Services, which already had a staff of four photographers. For six months Michelle shot pictures for the department without salary, waiting for a break. In January 1983, she was hired as a photographer for *Impact*, the department's monthly magazine. Her work got her noticed, and she was subsequently hired by Grayson Mitchell, an old friend from the *Daily News*, when Washington was elected mayor in April. Although she plans to stick with Mayor Washington during his term in office, Washington, D.C. is still part of her ambitions.

Michelle has been first in breaking two barriers. She is the first black female to be photographer for the mayor of the city of Chicago and the first black female to join the International Photographers of the Motion Picture and Television Industries Union. She also holds memberships in many noted professional organizations, such as the Chicago Association of Black Journalists, the National Association of Black Journalists, and the Chicago Press Photographers Association. Michelle's photographs have been published in *Ebony, Jet, The Chicago Tribune, The Chicago Sun Times, The New York Times*, The Associated Press, United Press International, and Wire Service Publications.

153. Michelle V. Agins at work. Bob Black, photographer

Photo by Michelle V. Agins, represented by the Hartman Group

Photo by Michelle V. Agins, represented by the Hartman Group

154. Mayor Harold Washington at a community forum

155. Mayor Harold Washington at a graduation. (The young man receiving the diploma had leukemia. He died two weeks after receiving his high school diploma.)

156. 'Twas the Night Before Christmas

157. McWashington (Mayor Harold Washington leads the St. Patrick's Day Parade)

Salimah Ali

Born in Harlem and raised in Brooklyn until age eleven, Salimah credits her father for her artistic talents. A graduate of the Fashion Institute of Technology, Salimah Ali earned a degree in fashion photography in 1977. She is a young working mother, whose work has been frequently exhibited in group showings throughout New York, such as at the Studio Museum in Harlem, the International Black Photographers exhibit, and the Black Enterprise Gallery. Salimah's other accomplishments include a position as staff photographer for Mel Wright Studios, assistant photographer for Leber Katz Advertising Studio, photo editor for *Encore* magazine, and the cover photograph for a book entitled *Sister Outsider*, by Audre Lorde.

She currently works as a freelance photographer and teaches photography full-time at the Jamaica Arts Center in Jamaica, New York.

Salimah Ali

158. Audre Lorde

Cary Beth Cryor

Cary Beth Cryor, born in Baltimore on November 19, 1947, has been a professional photographer for the past fifteen years. She received a B.S. degree in art education from Morgan State University in 1969. Upon graduation, Cary entered Pratt Institute in Brooklyn for graduate studies, where she earned her M.F.A. in photography in 1971. With the M.F.A. degree in hand, she entered the motion picture industry, where she worked for three years as a film editor, ending that career with the commercially successful film *Claudine*.

In 1979, Cary produced a powerful group of photographs that she took during the actual birth of her child. She comments, "These photographs were taken by me during labor, between contractions and during the actual delivery process. There are many feats in us and many challeges still to conquer. As unusual as this may appear, it was not difficult. It is my hope that this will serve as inspiration to other women who may want to do the unthinkable, the unfathomable, the utterly ridiculous."

The roles Cary plays are varied; however, she finds the role of parenting to be the most challenging. At the age of thirty-seven, she is currently an assistant professor of art at Coppin State College in Baltimore, where she teaches photography.

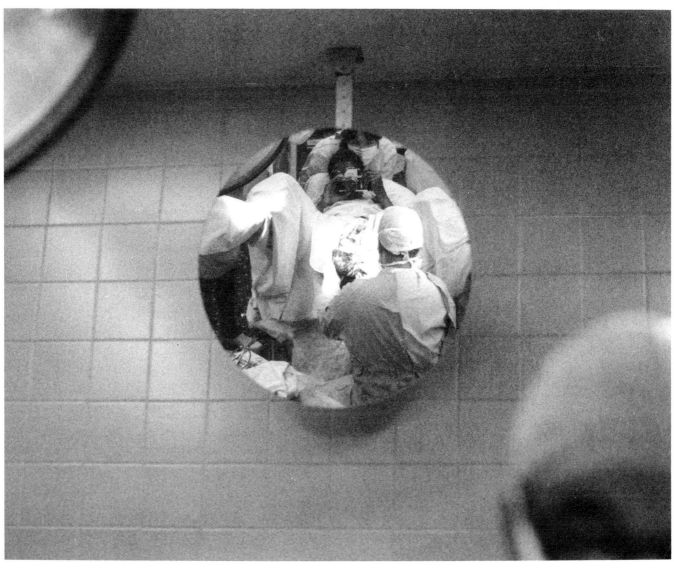

159. Rites of Passage #1

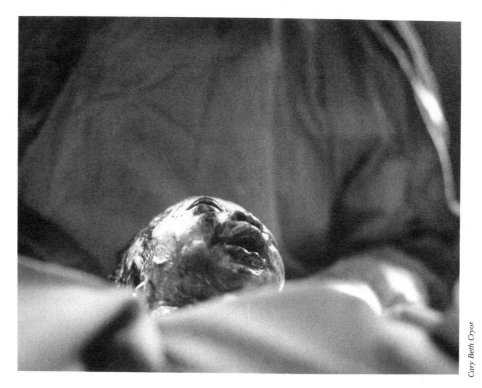

160. Rites of Passage #2

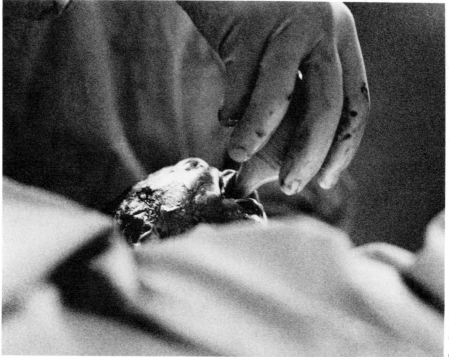

161. Rites of Passage #3

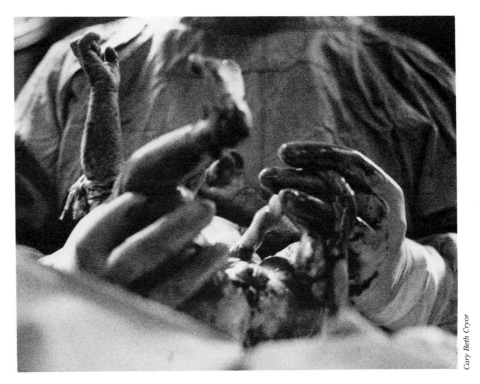

Cary Beth Cryor

162. Rites of Passage #4

Cary Beth Cryor

163. Rites of Passage #5

Lenore Davis

Lenore Davis of New York City is a graduate of the School of Visual Arts. She has exhibited at the Kodak Camera Club in Rochester and at the Women's Interart Center in Manhattan. In August 1973, she was featured as *Art Direction* magazine's "Upcoming Photographer" of the month.

In 1983, Lenore traveled to Thailand, where she photographed the surrender of the communist insurgents and sympathizers to the Thai army commander-in-chief. They were the last of the ten thousand rebels living in the hills of Mukdahan, the province bordering Laos. Lenore comments: "The soldiers still carried the Soviet weapons. Some were trained in Vietnam, China, and Laos, which is only a few miles from Mukdahan. They had been living in the jungle since 1965. Fighting and starving was their way of life. The surrender was a political media event. The rebels were paraded with red Chinese uniforms, flags, and machine guns. After the official surrender, their leaders carried photos of the royal family. After that, they were fed and they ate like animals who hadn't had enough food for years."

Lenore has worked as a photographer for *The Village Voice*. She is currently a staff photographer for the *New York Post*.

164.

165.

166.

167.

168.

169.

Julia Jones

Julia Jones studied photography formally under the direction of Wadsworth Jarrell and at the Howard University College of Fine Arts. She began her photography career in 1972 with the Howard University public relations office. For the past twelve years she has freelanced in the Washington, D.C., area. In December 1983, Julia accompanied the Reverend Jesse Jackson and his delegation of religious leaders to Syria on their mission to ask for the release of U. S. Navy flyer Robert Goodman. Her photos have been published in *U.S. News & World Report, Colorlines* magazine, *New Directions* magazine, and *The Afro-American* newspaper.

171. Jesse Jackson in Syria

Fern Logan

Fern Logan was born in Jamaica, New York, in July 1945. She attended Pratt Institute and majored in graphic arts. Photography had always been an interest, but it didn't become a passion for her until 1974, when she studied with Paul Caponigro at the Apeiron Workshop. She lists Caponigro as the major influence on her style and philosophy of photography as art. For ten years, as a single parent, she had to work full-time as a graphic designer in order to support her family and her habit—photography. In February 1983, Fern began to concentrate exclusively on photography and left her full-time job in the corporate world in order to begin her own photography and design business. She calls this decision the best one she ever made. She was the recipient of a 1984 New York State Council on the Arts Grant to continue an artist portrait series that she began in 1982. The February 1985 issue of *Popular Photography* did a profile on her and mentioned her one-woman show at the Cinque Gallery in New York City.

172. Millerton Station

173. Clouds

Akili-Casundria Ramsess

As a high school student in North Carolina, Akili-Casundria Ramsess served as photographer for the school newspaper and yearbook for three years. At that time she was primarily self-taught and learned as much as she could from books and magazines. "I was heavily inspired by the works of *Life*'s photographers Gordon Parks and Eugene Smith and FSA photographers of the 1930s."

After graduating from high school she moved to California and further pursued her studies in photography at Los Angeles Trade Technical College. She is currently completing a B.A. in photojournalism at California State University in Long Beach while pursuing work as a freelance photographer in the local newspaper market, primarily the *Los Angeles Times*. Even though she photographs a variety of subjects, her greatest interest is in photographing people.

174. Guitar player

Akili-Casundria Ramsess

175. Peanut man

Coreen Simpson

I like flamboyance and excessiveness—those things that seem off," says Coreen Simpson. That remark sums up her work as much as anything can. Originally a writer, she became disillusioned with the photographs other people were taking to illustrate her articles and decided that she could do better. One thing led to another, and eventually Coreen was getting more requests for her photographic services than for her writing.

Coreen shoots with a wide-angle lens and direct flash, and produces images that make her subjects leap out at the viewer. Her freelance work frequently appears in *The New York Amsterdam News,* the *New York Post, The Village Voice, Black Enterprise, Encore,* and *Essence.* Her photographs were also published in the photographic essay "Harlem on My Mind," re-released in 1979.

Coreen recently completed work on a documentary film about the Chelsea Hotel in New York City for the British Broadcasting Corporation. She has had one-person exhibitions at the Brooklyn Museum and the Addison Green Gallery and has participated in group exhibitions at several other galleries. She was assistant curator of photography and staff photographer at the Studio Museum of Harlem in 1978. Her work is represented in the collections of the Harlem State Office Building, the International Center for Photography, the James Van Der Zee Institute, and the Schomburg Center for Research in Black Culture.

176. Untitled   *Coreen Simpson*

177. Untitled   *Coreen Simpson*

178. Untitled   *Coreen Simpson*

179. Untitled   *Coreen Simpson*

Leah Ann Washington

Leah Ann Washington was born in New Orleans, Louisiana, where her mother, Adine Williams, owned and operated a photographic studio. Although Leah attended Southern University in Baton Rouge, she later enrolled at Brooks Institute of Photography, where she became that school's first black woman graduate.

Leah's mother, Adine Williams, said, "I guess Leah was destined to work in photography. The very night she was born, I worked in the darkroom processing film and making prints, just before being taken to the hospital for her delivery. She was born into photography." Leah has two brothers who are both photographers too, and her parents continue to run a successful studio in Baton Rouge. Leah is currently a wife, a mother, and a working photographer, now residing in Monterey, California.

Leah Washington

180. Portrait

Leah Washington

181. Point Lobos—at Carmel, California

Bio-Bibliography

1860–1900

BAKER, HATTIE   active 1887
Cleveland, Ohio

This photographer worked as a specialist in photographic enlargements. An advertisement describing her specialty appears in *The Cleveland Gazette*, January 15, 1887, page 4, columns 1 and 2.

FLENOY, MARY E.   active 1893–1909
Danville, Illinois

Flenoy is listed in the Danville city directory. Her studios, at 613 South Street and 106 North Washington Avenue, appear in the directory in 1893, 1899, 1903, 1904, 1905, and 1906. Flenoy was the only photographer attending the National Negro Business League Convention, which was held in Indianapolis in 1904.

Source: National Negro Business League Proceedings, Volumes 5 and 6.

THOMPSON, FANNY J.   active 1880s
Memphis, Tennessee

Thompson devoted her school vacation to the study of photography. Besides photography, Thompson was a noted musician and composer. A musical piece that she composed, entitled "Fond Memories," was published by the editor of *The Cleveland Gazette*. She was often mentioned on the society pages of the *Gazette*.

Sources: *Cleveland Gazette*: January 17, 1885: page 4, column 1.
    Cleveland Gazette: February 20, 1886: page 4, column 3.
    Cleveland Gazette: May 22, 1886: page 1, column 1.

WARREN, MARY E.   active 1866
Houston, Texas

Warren is listed in the Houston city directory as a photographic printer.

1900–1940

ALLEN, WINIFRED HALL   active 1930s
New York, New York

Allen was born in Jamaica, West Indies. She moved to New York City at the age of eighteen and worked as an apprentice to William Woodard in his photograph studio at 2386 Seventh Avenue. Allen is a graduate of the New York Institute of Photography. She also maintained a studio at 311 W. 141 Street, New York, New York.

Source: *Harlem As Is*: 1936–1937.

BROWN, ALBERTA H.   active 1930s–1940s
Richmond, Virginia

The Browns owned and operated the Brown Studio, serving the black community of Richmond. Brown did some studio work, which included the hand tinting of photographs. Most of her photographic work was done outside the studio, where she took class pictures for some of Richmond's black schools.

Source: 1934–1935 Richmond city directory.

CALLOWAY, LUCY   active 1920s
New York, New York

Calloway is listed in the 1922 New York city directory as a photographer. She exhibited two photographs at the New York Public Library, Negro Division, at 103 West 135th Street. The exhibition was curated by bibliophile and collector Arthur A. Schomburg.

Source: Exhibition catalog: "Negro Arts Exhibit," the New York Public Library, Negro Division, August 1–September 30, 1921.

MRS. COLLINS   active 1920s–1930s
New Orleans, Louisiana

Collins owned and operated the Collins studio on South Rampart Street.

Source: New Orleans city directory

HARLESTON, ELISE FORREST   active 1919–1920s
Charleston, South Carolina

Elise Forrest Harleston was married to portrait and genre painter Edwin Harleston. Before her marriage, Elise studied photography. In 1919, she enrolled at the E. Brunel School of Photography in New York City. She later studied at Tuskegee Institute and was an apprentice to C. M. Battey, who was head of the photographic division (1915–1927). She returned to Charleston and opened a studio with her husband at 118 Calhoun Street. Elise would photograph Edwin's subjects so they wouldn't have to pose motionless for hours, and Edwin would use the portraits to paint from. She died in 1971.

Sources: *Who's Who in Colored America*, 1922.
    Simms Blue Book, Chicago, 1923 (advertisement)
    Black Photographers 1840–1940: A Bio-Bibliography by Deborah Willis-Thomas.

LEWIS, GERTRUDE   active 1920s
Houston, Texas

Lewis is listed as a photographer in the Houston city directory. Her studio was located at 2307 Dowling Street.

ROBERTS, WILHELMINA   active 1920s–1930s
PEARL SELENA
Columbia, South Carolina

Wilhelmina Pearl Selena Williams Roberts was born in 1887. She attended Benedict College in Columbia but did not have formal training in photography. The mother of eight children, Wilhelmina assisted her photographer-husband Richard at the Roberts' Art Studio at 1119 Washington Street, Columbia.

Source: *Southern Indicator*, July 2, 1921 (advertisement).

ROBESON, ESLANDA   active 1920s–1950s
CARDOZA GOODE
New York, New York

The daughter of John and Eslanda (Cardoza) Goode, Robeson was a woman of many talents. She studied at the State University in Illinois for three years. She earned her B.S. from Columbia University and studied at Columbia University Medical School for one year. She was the first black to be employed on the staff of Columbia Presbyterian Hospital, where she was a chemist and technician in charge of the Surgical Pathological Laboratory. She later managed the career of her husband, Paul Robeson. It was during this period that she began photographing her famous husband's life-style and the distinguished people she met in her travels. From 1935–1937 she studied anthropology at the London School of Economics. She published three books: *African Journey*, a book that chronicles her journey to Africa in 1936 with photographs; *Paul Robeson, Negro*; and *What Do The People of Africa Want?* She was also the mother of one son, Paul Robeson, Jr. Eslanda Robeson died in 1965 of cancer.

Sources: *New York Herald Tribune*, August 13, 1945
    New York Times, August 9, 1945.
    African Journey, by Eslanda Goode Robeson (The John Day Company, New York, 1945).

SHUMATE, HAZEL   active 1930s–1940s
Los Angeles, California

Shumate was born in 1915 and began working as a freelance photographer in the late 1930s.

Source: *Ebony*, February 1950, p. 73.

TEAL, ELNORA   active 1919–1960s
Houston, Texas

Teal learned photography from her photographer-husband, Arthur Chester Teal. The studio, the Teal Portrait Studio, on Milam Street, was located in the heart of downtown Houston. Teal worked out of that studio, while her husband spent most of his time at their other studio on Dowling Street. Teal was very busy at the Milam Street studio because she used the finest materials for her work and had a good sense for portraiture, which made her very popular with her clientele.

WELCOME, JENNIE LOUISE   active 1910–1920s
VAN DER ZEE
New York, New York

Welcome was born on January 10, 1885, in Lenox, Massachusetts. She was educated at Lenox High School.

She was the sister of photographer James Van Der Zee, who chronicled Harlem and its residents for over fifty years. She taught classes in the Toussaint Conservatory of Art and Music, 253 West 134th Street, New York City, which was owned by Welcome and her husband, Ernest Toussaint Welcome. The classes she taught were in art, music, and photography. There was also a photographic studio in the conservatory.

Sources: *Crisis*, December 1910.
    Who's Who in Colored America, 1929.

WILLIAMS, ADINE   active 1936 to the present
Baton Rouge, Louisiana

Williams is the owner of the Picture Place, a photo studio in Baton Rouge. She is the former owner of Camera Masters in New Orleans and Camera Masters in Monterey, California.

1940–1960

ALLEN, GLADYS   active 1940s to the present
Los Angeles, California

Allen is currently operating the Gladys Allen photography studio in Los Angeles. She has been an active photographer for over thirty years. Her subject matter ranges from children to weddings to celebrities.

AUGUSTUS, CAROL   active 1940s
Wilmington, North Carolina

Augustus was co-operator of the Vanderbilt Studio, Ninth and Castle Streets, Wilmington, during the 1940s.

Sources: *Negro Business and Professional Men and Women, A Survey of Business in North Carolina*, Volume 2, 1946, by Irving Boone.

BOMAR, JOHNNIE MAE   active 1940s–1950s
Akron, Ohio

Bomar achieved national prominence when she won the Ohio Shriners beauty contest at Cleveland in 1948 and went on to represent Ohio in the finals. Bomar had been a professional photographer for three years in November 1949.

Source: *Color*, November 1949, p. 16.

BROOKS, CHARLOTTE   active 1940s
Cleveland, Ohio

Brooks was a freelance photographer for *Our World* magazine.

Source: *Our World*, May 1946, p. 6.

CHARLOTTE   active 1950s
New York, New York

Charlotte is listed in a 1951 New York Negro Business Directory as a photographer.

CHUR, HELEN JONES   active 1940s
Chicago, Illinois

Chur is listed as a photographer in the exhibition catalogue, "A Century of Black Photographers," Rhode Island School of Design, 1983.

DAVIS, BILLIE   active 1940s–1950s
LOUISE BARBOUR
Hampton, Virginia

Davis was born in Kansas City, Missouri, in 1906. She was the mother of three children and studied photography with Hampton Institute's photography instructor, Ruben Burrell. Her husband, Collis, was a professor and the dean of students at Hampton Institute. She died of arteriosclerosis in 1955.

DORSEY, THEODORA   active 1940s
Los Angeles, California

Dorsey owned and operated the Theodora Dorsey Studio of Photography in Los Angeles during the 1940s.

Source: *Home Circuit*, May 1947, p. 3.

DOWNS, EMMA ALICE   active 1940s

Sergeant Downs was an official WAC staff photographer.

Source: Green, Robert Ewell, *Black Defenders of America*, 1775–1973 (Chicago: Johnson Publishing Company, 1974.)

GUY, EDNA   active 1940s

Guy was a freelance photographer for *Our World* magazine.

Source: *Our World*, April 1946, p. 6.

HARDISON, INGE   active 1950s–1960s
New York, New York

A native of Portsmouth, Virginia, Hardison attended the Art Student's League in New York City, where she studied painting, sculpture and photography. During the 1950s she worked as a freelance photographer selling her stories and pictures to various publications.

Source: *EBONY Success Library, Vol 1, 1000 Successful Blacks*, Nashville, Tenn., 1973 by arrangement with Johnson Publishing Company.

HOOD, ZEBONIA   active 1950s
Atlanta, Georgia

Hood had a photo studio at 616 Fair Avenue, N.E., in Atlanta for a number of years.

HOWARD, A. GRENDEL   active 1960s–1970s
Master Sergeant

WAC professional photographer M. Sgt. Grendel Howard went into the army with a background in advertising and marketing. Selected many times as Outstanding WAC during her first assignment (as editor of her installation newspaper), she quit the army for three years to continue her college studies.

After Vietnam, where she was awarded the Bronze Star, Howard returned to the States and adopted a three-year-old boy, making her one of the first single WACs to adopt a child. From 1974 to 1976, she worked in the TRADOC Public Affairs Office at Fort Monroe, in Hampton, Virginia.

Source: *Casemate Chronicle*, June 1977.

JACKSON, ANN ELIZABETH   active 1940s
Columbus, Ohio

Jackson was born in 1922 and was the only woman photographer employed by the Veterans Administration in Columbus in the 1950s. Specializing in high-quality copy work, she made reproductions of X-rays and other medical documents, which were shipped to Veterans Administration physicians and private hospitals all over the country. An ex-fashion designer and government clerk, Jackson was assistant photographer specializing in line copy work before joining the Veterans Administration staff. She also worked as a freelance press and portrait photographer. She also worked in large-format, eight-by-ten camera work.

Source: *Ebony*, March 1955, p. 5.

JACKSON, VERA   active 1930s to the present
Los Angeles, California

Jackson was born in Wichita, Kansas, in 1912. She worked as a photographer for *The California Eagle* in the 1940s. During those years she photographed many of the black entertainers who were in the Los Angeles area. Jackson is an exhibiting photographer and painter.

JEFFERSON, LOUISE   active 1940s to the present
New York, New York
Litchfield, Connecticut

Jefferson is a member of the Photographic Society of America, the American Institute of Graphic Arts, the Executive Committee of the Women's Africa Committee, and is a consultant to the Gallery of Modern Art in New York. In addition to being a photographer, she is a writer, graphic artist, and illustrator. Jefferson studied fine arts at Hunter College and graphic arts at Columbia University. She has recently been honored by the Connecticut Historical Society in appreciation of her work. She is a member of the Alpha Kappa Alpha sorority and a consultant. She is best known as an illustrator. Presently, she is doing photographic work for a book about the Buell family, early settlers of Litchfield, Connecticut. She is also doing research on Scandinavian countries for a publishing firm.

Sources: *Johnson Press Chronicle*, May 1980, p. 28.
Hartford Courant, February 5, 1984, p. E10.
Trinity Tripod, February 1982.
The Decorative Arts of Africa, by Louise Jefferson.
The Litchfield Enquirer, January 31, 1980.

Exhibitions: Baltimore Museum of Art; Schomburg Center; the New York Public Library; the Craftery Gallery, among others.

JOHNSON, MARJORIE   active 1940s
Boston, Massachusetts

Johnson was born in North Carolina in 1918. She has worked as a photographer, beautician, interior decorator, and mortician.

Source: *Ebony*, August 1959, p. 53.

LOVELACE, MARIE   active 1930s–1970s
Chicago, Illinois

Lovelace is listed as a photographer in the exhibition catalogue *A Century of Black Photographers.*

MARTIN, LOUISE OZELL   active 1930s–1970s
Houston, Texas

Martin was born in Brenham, Texas, on January 9, 1914. She is a graduate of Denver University and is the proprietor of the Louise Martin Art Studio and the Louise Martin School of Photography in Houston.

Sources: *The Houston Chronicle*, June 12, 1969, p. 5.
The Houston Informer, February 16, 1965, p. 6.
The Houston Post, February 12, 1984, p. 4G.

MAYO, LYDIA   active 1940s
Wilmington, North Carolina

Mayo was co-operator of the Vanderbilt Studio in Wilmington.

Source: *Negro Business and Professional Men and Women, A Survey of Business in North Carolina*, Volume 2, 1946, by Irving Boone.

MILLER, DORA   active 1940s–1950s
Los Angeles, California

Miller was born in Oklahoma City. She was a graduate of the California School of Photography. She assisted in operating the Avalon Photography Studio in Los Angeles. Miller died of a heart attack at the age of thirty-three in 1951.

MILLER, LAVINIA C.   active 1940s–1960s
North Carolina

Miller served in the WACs as a photographer and then attended the New Haven School of Photography before going on to work as a freelancer in Washington. She was hired by the Pathology Institute's Photography Division in 1950 and then made medical photographer on the recommendation of her supervisor.

Source: *Ebony*, February 1961, p. 6.

SIMPSON, MARIE C.   active 1940s–1950s
Birmingham, Alabama

Simpson is listed as a photographer in the 1941 Birmingham city directory.

WASHINGTON, RUTH BRUMMEL   active 1940s
Los Angeles, California

Born in 1914, Washington owned and operated the Avalon Photography studio in the 1940s. In 1943, she married Leon H. Washington, publisher of *The Los Angeles Sentinel.* According to an article published in *Ebony* in 1975, "In 1948, [her husband] had a stroke which left him unable to carry on the day-to-day work of running a newspaper. . . . Ruth, a studio photographer, decided that she would take over even though she didn't know anything about the news business. 'I surrounded myself with good professionals,' she says, 'top journalists and other people.' Today the weekly *Sentinel* is one of the leaders among black newspapers in real estate and classified ads. The size of the paper has more than doubled."

Source: *Ebony*, November, 1975, p. 108.

WILLIAMS, ELIZABETH "TEX"   active 1940s–1970s
Houston, Texas

Williams was a WAC photographer for the U.S. Army in 1944. In 1940 she was an assistant to Stanley Reddick at the Stanley Reddick Art Studio in Houston. She was the first black woman to graduate from the Fort Monmouth, New Jersey, Photo School. Her work included public relations, medical photography, army maneuvers, and ID pictures. She also did pictures for the defense intelligence agencies, local and post newspapers. Williams retired from the army in 1971.

WILSON, JOYCE R.   active 1940s
New York, New York
Mill Valley, California

Wilson worked as a portrait and fine art photographer in New York City. She moved to California in the 1950s.

WOODWARD, EMMA KING   active 1940s
Dallas, Texas

Woodward worked as a photographer in Texas during the 1940s.

Sources: *The Negro in Texas History, 1836–1936.* (souvenir of the Texas Centennial)
      Negro Business Directory of Dallas, Texas, 1947–48.

WORTHINGTON, ETHEL   active 1940s
Chicago, Illinois

Worthington, of the Worthington Studio in Chicago, took over her husband's business when he died in the 1930s and continued running their studio through the 1940s. She is listed as a photographer in the exhibition catalogue *A Century of Black Photographers*.

General Listing:
1860–1960

ALLEN, GLADYS

ALLEN, WINIFRED HALL

AUGUSTUS, CAROL

BAKER, HATTIE

BOMAR, JOHNNIE MAE

BROOKS, CHARLOTTE

BROWN, ALBERTA H.

CALLOWAY, LUCY

CHARLOTTE

CHUR, HELEN JONES

COLLINS, MRS.

DAVIS, BILLIE LOUISE BARBOUR

DORSEY, THEODORA

DOWNS, Sgt. EMMA ALICE

FLENOY, MARY E.

GUY, EDNA

HARDISON, INGE

HARLESTON, ELISE FORREST

HOOD, ZEBONIA

HOWARD, M. Sgt. A. GRENDEL

JACKSON, ANN ELIZABETH

JACKSON, VERA

JEFFERSON, LOUISE

JOHNSON, MARJORIE

LEWIS, GERTRUDE

LOVELACE, MARIE

MARTIN, LOUISE OZELL

MAYO, LYDIA

MILLER, DORA

MILLER, LAVINIA C.

ROBERTS, WILHELMINA PEARL SELENA

ROBESON, ESLANDA CARDOZA GOODE

SHUMATE, HAZEL

SIMPSON, MARIE C.

TEAL, ELNORA

THOMPSON, FANNY J.

WARREN, MARY E.

WASHINGTON, RUTH B. BRUMMEL

WELCOME, JENNIE LOUISE

WILLIAMS, ADINE

WILLIAMS, ELIZABETH "TEX"

WILSON, JOYCE R.

WOODWARD, EMMA KING

WORTHINGTON, ETHEL

General Listing:
1960–1980

AGINS, MICHELLE

ALI, SALIMAH

ANDERSON, ESTHER

ASBURY, DANA

BARNES, DONNA MARIE

BELL-TAITT, CAROLYN

BLALOCK, ELLEN

BLUE, CAROL PARROTT

BOND, SANDRA TURNER

BRISSETT, BONNIE

BROOKS, QUEEN E.

BURNS, MILLIE

CAMPBELL, MICHELLE

CLARKE, MARNA

COLE, JUANITA

COLLINS, BONNIE

CRYOR, CARY BETH

DAVIS, LENORE

DAVIS, PAT

DE LEON, PERLA

DUMETZ, BARBARA

FARMER, SHARON

FARRIS, PHOEBE

FAULKNER, ANNA

FERRILL, MIKKI

FOURNIER, COLLETTE V.

GIRAUX, LEISANT

GLOSTER, DOROTHY

GUMS, LUCY

GUY, ROSALIND

HACKER, SUSAN

HAMLIN, ELLA

HAMMOND, LYDIA

HANSBERRY, GAIL ADELLE

HODGE, ADELLE

JONES, JULIA

LOGAN, FERN

MANN, AUGUSTA

MONTOUTE, MARLENE

MOORE, DIAN

MOORE, SHELLEY

MOUTOUSSAMY-ASHE, JEANNE

MUNGIN, CAROL

NANCE, MARILYN

PATTEN, JACQUELINE LAVETTA

PHILLIPS, GWEN

PHIPPS, PATRICIA

PREACELY, DIANE LOUISE

RAGLAND-NJAU, PHILLDA

RAMSESS, AKILI-CASUNDRIA

RAY, DEBORAH

REYNOLDS, SEAN

RICHARDSON, DEBBIE

ROBINSON, JOHNNIE DELL

SCHMERL, RENNIE

SIMONETTI, NAOMI

SIMPSON, COREEN

SIMPSON, LORNA

SMITH, MING

SOHAM, KALIMA

STEPHENS, JOAN BYRD

STEWART, JO MOORE

STRADFORD, LAUREL

TAYLOR, KATHLEEN-MARIE

TAYLOR, KAY

TEASDALE, ROSETTA C.

TOMLIN, ELAINE

WASHINGTON, LEAH ANN

WASHINGTON, RUBY

WATSON, SHARON

WEEMS, CARRIE

WHITE, JUDITH

WILLIS-RYAN, DEBORAH

WILSON, DELCINA

Geographical Index

1860–1960

ALABAMA, Birmingham — Marie C. Simpson

CALIFORNIA, Los Angeles
- Gladys Allen
- Theodora Dorsey
- Vera Jackson
- Dora Miller
- Hazel Shumate
- Ruth B. Washington
- Joyce R. Wilson

Mill Valley

GEORGIA, Atlanta — Zebonia Hood

ILLINOIS, Chicago
- Helen Jones Chur
- Marie Lovelace
- Ethel Worthington
- Mary E. Flenoy

Danville

LOUISIANA, Baton Rouge
New Orleans
- Adine Williams
- Mrs. Collins

MASSACHUSETTS, Boston — Marjorie Johnson

NEW YORK, New York
- Winifred Hall Allen
- Lucy Calloway
- Emma Alice Downs
- Inge Hardison
- Louise Jefferson
- Eslanda Cardoza Goode Robeson
- Jennie Louise Welcome

NORTH CAROLINA, Wilmington
- Carol Augustus
- Lydia Mayo

OHIO, Akron
Columbus
Cleveland
- Johnnie Mae Bomar
- Ann Elizabeth Jackson
- Hattie Baker
- Charlotte Brooks

SOUTH CAROLINA, Charleston
Columbia
- Elise Forrest Harleston
- Wilhelmina Pearl Selena Roberts

TENNESSEE, Memphis — Fanny J. Thompson

TEXAS, Dallas
Houston
- Emma King Woodward
- Gertrude Lewis
- Louise Martin
- Elnora Teal
- Mary E. Warren
- Elizabeth "Tex" Williams

VIRGINIA, Hampton
Richmond
- Billie Louise Barbour Davis
- Alberta H. Brown

1960–1980

CALIFORNIA, Berkeley
    Los Angeles — Mikki Ferrill, Carol Parrott Blue, Barbara DuMetz, Debbie Richardson, Gwen Phillips, Akili-Casundria Ramsess

    Monterey — Leah Ann Washington

    San Francisco — Sean Reynolds, Carrie Weems

CONNECTICUT, Hartford — Marna Clark, Kathleen-Marie Taylor, Kay Taylor

DISTRICT OF COLUMBIA — Sandra Turner Bond, Sharon Farmer, Phoebe Farris, Gail Adelle Hansberry, Julia Jones

GEORGIA, Atlanta — Jo Moore Stewart

ILLINOIS, Chicago — Michelle Agins, Adelle Hodge, Diane Louise Preacely, Laurel Stradford

MARYLAND, Baltimore — Cary Beth Cryor

MICHIGAN, Detroit — Anna Faulkner, Deborah Ray

MISSOURI, St. Louis — Susan Hacker

NEW MEXICO, Albuquerque — Dana Asbury

NEW JERSEY, Hoboken — Naomi Simonetti
    Plainfield — Phillda Ragland-Njau

NEW YORK, Brooklyn — Millie Burns, Leisant Giraux, Ella Hamlin, Dian Moore, Shelley Moore, Marilyn Nance, Ruby Washington

    Bronx — Jacqueline LaVetta Patten

    Mt. Vernon — Carol Mungin
    New York — Salimah Ali, Donna Marie Barnes, Juanita Cole, Lenore Davis, Pat Davis, Perla De Leon, Dorothy Gloster, Lydia Hammond, Gail Adelle Hansberry, Fern Logan, Augusta Mann, Marlene Montoute, Jeanne Moutoussamy-Ashe, Patricia Phipps, Coreen Simpson, Lorna Simpson, Ming Smith, Joan Byrd Stephens, Deborah Willis-Ryan

    Rochester — Bonnie Brissett, Collette V. Fournier
    Syracuse — Ellen Blalock

OHIO, Columbus — Queen E. Brooks

PENNSYLVANIA, Pittsburgh — Sharon Watson

TEXAS, Austin — Michelle Campbell

Footnotes

[1] Brabara Gamarekian, "Black Women Emerge from History's Neglect," *New York Times,* March 6, 1985, p. 6.

[2] Lee Kravitz, "On Camera; Photography as Art," *Signature* (August 1984): pp. 4–8.

[3] Valencia Hollins Coar, *A Century of Black Photographers: 1840–1860* (Providence, Rhode Island: Rhode Island School of Design, Museum of Art, 1983), p. 9.

[4] "Photographic Instrument for Sale," *Weekly Anglo-African* (January 14, 1860): p. 3.

[5] Conversation with Deborah Willis-Ryan, photograph specialist at the Schomburg Center for Research in Black Culture, New York City.

[6] W. A. Low and Virgil A. Clift, eds., *Encyclopedia of Black America* (New York: McGraw-Hill, 1981), p. 332.

[7] Ibid., pp. 118–19.

[8] M. A. Majors, *Noted Negro Women, Their Triumphs and Activities* (Chicago: Donohue and Henneberry, 1893), pp. 27–30.

[9] Vishnu V. Oak, *The Negro Adventure in General Business* (Yellow Springs, Ohio: Antioch Press, 1949), pp. 30–31.

[10] Martin V. Sandler, *The Story of American Photography* (Boston: Little Brown and Company, 1979), p. 20.

[11] Ibid., p. 17.

[12] Dorothy Sterling, *We Are Your Sisters: Black Women in the Nineteenth Century* (New York, W. W. Norton, 1984), p. 19.

[13] Bert James Loewenberg and Ruth Bogin, eds., *Black Women in Nineteenth-Century American Life* (Penn State University Press, 1976), pp. 63–69.

[14] Ibid.

[15] Clift and Low, *Encyclopedia of Black America*, pp. 117–19.

[16] U. S., Bureau of the Census, *1850 Census Report* (Washington: Government Printing Office, 1853).

[17] William Loren Katz, ed., *Negro Population in the United States 1790–1915* (New York: Arno Press and The New York Times, 1968).

[18] Ibid., pp. 27–28.

[19] Oak, *Negro Adventure in General Business*, p. 38.

[20] Ibid., p. 40.

[21] George E. Haynes, *The Negro at Work in New York City* (New York: AMS Press, 1968), p. 94.

[22] Oak, *Negro Adventure in General Business*, p. 41.

[23] Houston City Directory, 1866.

[24] Haynes, *The Negro at Work in New York City*, pp. 15–17.

[25] Ibid., p. 27.

[26] U. S., Bureau of the Census, *1870 Census Report* (Washington: Government Printing Office, 1872).

[27] Sandler, *Story of American Photography*, p. 30.

28 "Artists of the Bowery," *New York Times*, April 12, 1885, p. 14.

29 "The Real Cause," *New York Times*, February 23, 1884, p. 4.

30 "Photography and Black-mail," *New York Times*, April 21, 1883, pp. 1–2.

31 "Photographed While Kissing," *New York Times*, April 21, 1883, p. 2.

32 *Cleveland Gazette*, May 22, 1886, p. 1.

33 Ibid.

34 *Cleveland Gazette*, January 15, 1887, p. 4.

35 Katz, *Negro Population in the United States 1790-1915*, p. 527.

36 J. R. Hamm, *National Negro Business League Proceedings* (Boston: 1900), p. 23.

37 Margaret Bisland, "Women and Their Cameras," *Outing* (October 17, 1890): pp. 36–43.

38 Clarence B. Moore, "Women Experts in Photography," *Cosmopolitan* (March 1893): pp. 580–90.

39 "Women Who Press the Button," *New York Times*, October 1, 1893, p. 18.

40 Hamm, *National Negro Business League Proceedings*, p. 23.

41 "The Negro at Paris in 1900," *Kansas City Observer*, January 27, 1900.

42 U. S., Bureau of the Census, *1900 Census Report* (Washington: Government Printing Office, 1902), p. 527.

43 Andrew Hilyer, *20th Century Union League Directory* (Washington, D.C.), pp. 107–11.

44 W. W. Holland, "Photography for Our Young People," *Colored American* (May 1902): pp. 5-9.

45 Fannie B. Williams, "The Colored Girl," *Voice of the Negro* (June 1905): pp. 400–403.

46 J. R. Hamm, *National Negro Business League Proceedings*, Indianapolis: 1904.

47 J. R. Hamm, *National Negro Business League Proceedings*, New York City: 1905.

48 Louis R. Harlan and Raymond W. Smock, *The Booker T. Washington Papers 1901-1902* (Urbana: University of Illinois Press, 1972), pp. 501–2.

49 Ibid.

50 Ibid., p. 504.

51 Haynes, *The Negro at Work in New York City*, pp. 124–26.

52 Katz, *Negro Population in the United States 1790–1915*, p. 51.

53 Ibid., p. 510.

54 U. S., Bureau of the Census, *1910 Census Report* (Washington: Government Printing Office, 1913).

55 *Crisis* (December 1910): inside front cover.

56 Florette Henri, *Black Migration: Movement North, 1900–1920* (New York: Anchor Press/Double Day, 1976), p. 141.

57 Ibid., p. 168.

58 Quoted in Sandler, *The Story of American Photography*, pp. 104–5.

59 Helmut Gernsheim and Alison Gernsheim, *A Concise History of Photography* (London: Thames and Hudson, 1965), pp. 191–202.

60 U. S., Bureau of the Census, *1920 Census Report* (Washington: Government Printing Office, Population), p. 357.

61 "Occupational Classes Among Negroes in Cities," *American Journal of Sociology* (March 1930): pp. 718–38.

62 Hamm, *National Negro Business League Proceedings*, Indianapolis, p. 68.

63 Ibid., pp. 68–78.

64 Ibid.

65 Sadie T.M. Alexander, "Negro Women in our Economic Life," *Opportunity* (July 1930), pp. 201–3.

66 Letter from Elise Harleston to Edwin Harleston, New York, New York, September 15, 1919.

67 *Tuskegee Student*, December 17, 1921.

68 Personal interview with Wilhelmena Wynn, daughter of photographer, New York, New York, December 11, 1984.

69 Personal interview with Lucille Moore, assistant to the Teals, Houston, Texas, January 7, 1985.

70 U. S., Bureau of the Census, *1930 Census Report* (Washington: Government Printing Office, 1983).

71 Katz, *Negro Population in the United States, 1790–1915*, p. 324.

72 U. S., Women's Bureau, *Women's Job Advances and Growth* (Washington: Government Printing Office, 1949).

[73] Oak, *Negro Adventure in General Business*, p. 49.

[74] St. Clair Drake and Horace R. Cayton, *Black Metropolis* (New York: Harcourt Brace and Company, 1945), p. 220.

[75] Benjamin Quarles, *The Negro in the Making of America* (New York: Collier Books, 1969), p. 204.

[76] Ibid., 201.

[77] Myrtle Evangeline Pollard, *Harlem As Is*, New York: City University of New York Thesis, 1936.

[78] *New York Times*, February 2, 1936, p. 11.

[79] Oak, *Negro Adventure in General Business*, p. 48.

[80] "Teachers in an Army School," *New York Times*, October 17, 1943.

[81] "Future Predicted for Women Fliers," *New York Times*, November 2, 1944.

[82] "It's a Women's War, Too," *New York Times*, January 10, 1943, Sec. 2, p. 2.

[83] "Candies Liked in Italy," *New York Times*, December 29, 1943, p. 3.

[84] U. S., Women's Bureau, *Changes in Women's Occupations, 1940–1950* (Washington: Government Printing Office, 1954).

[85] Ibid.

[86] "Box Camera Lead," *New York Times*, September 24, 1950, Sec. 2, p. 15.

[87] Ibid., p. 12.

[88] U. S., Women's Bureau, *Changes in Women's Occupations, 1940–1950*.

[89] Pearl S. Buck and Eslanda Robeson, *American Argument* (New York: John Day Company, 1949), p. 16.

[90] Ibid., p. 25.

[91] Ibid.

[92] Ibid., pp. 12–13.

[93] Mable Smythe, ed., *The Black American Reference Book* (Englewood Cliffs, New Jersey: Prentice-Hall, 1976), p. 197.

[94] U. S., Bureau of the Census, *1950 Census Report*, Special Reports (Washington: Government Printing Office, 1952), pp. 113–15, table 1.

[95] Ibid., pp. 1B–29.

[96] U. S., Women's Bureau, *Negro Women and Their Jobs*.

[97] U. S., Bureau of the Census, *Census of Business 1954* (Washington: Government Printing Office, 1958), pp. 1–8, table 1D.

[98] Marjorie McKenzie, "In Fifty Years, Women Move Forward in Arts and Professions," *Pittsburgh Courier*, January 27, 1951.

[99] "Cited by Urban League," *New York Times*, May 1, 1955, p. 78.

[100] Ibid.

[101] Roscoe C. Brown, Jr., and Harry A. Ploski, *The Negro Almanac* (New York: Bellwether Publishing Company, 1967), p. 23.

[102] Phyllis A. Wallace, *Black Women in the Labor Force* (Cambridge: MIT Press, 1980), p. 7.

[103] U. S., Bureau of the Census, *1960 Census Report*, Special Studies (Washington: Government Printing Office, 1963), p. 22, table 3.

[104] U. S., Bureau of the Census, *Census of Business 1963* (Washington: Government Printing Office, 1965), pp. 1–7, table 1.

[105] Personal interview with Louise Martin, photographer, Houston, Texas, October, 1984.

[106] "Louise Martin: Giving It Her Best Shot," *Houston Post*, February 12, 1984, p. 4G.

[107] Personal interview with Louise Martin, photographer, Houston, Texas, October 1984.

[108] "Louise Martin: Giving It Her Best Shot," p. 4G.

[109] "Houston's Lady Photographer," *Houston Informer*, February 16, 1965, p. 6.

[110] "Louise Martin: Giving It Her Best Shot," p. 4G.

[111] "Houston's Leading Black Woman," *Houston Chronicle*, June 12, 1969, Sec. 2, p. 5.

[112] "Have Camera Will Travel," *Ebony*, March 1969, pp. 112–20.

[113] Clift and Low, *The Encyclopedia of Black America*, p. 356.

[114] "Aide Says Polaroid Move to Help South African Blacks is Success," *New York Times*, October 31, 1971, p. 12.

[115] Ibid.

[116] U. S., Bureau of the Census, *1970 Census Report* (Washington: Government Printing Office, 1972).

[117] "Along With The Three R's—Photography," *New York Times*, November 21, 1971, Sec. 2, p. 30.

[118] Ibid.

[119] Ibid.

[120] Jonathan Green, *American Photography: A Critical History 1945 to the Present* (New York: Harry Abrams, 1984), p. 89.

[121] Ibid., p. 15.

[122] Beaumont Newhall, *The History of Photography* (New York: Museum of Modern Art, 1964).

[123] Joe Crawford, ed., *The Black Photographers Annual.* Vols. 1–4. (Brooklyn, New York: Another View, 1971–1977).

[124] "Life May Have Died But Photography Lives on," *New York Times*, January 14, 1973, Sec. 2, p. 29.

[125] Ibid.

[126] *New York Times*, October 12, 1975, p. 11.

[127] *New York Times*, February 25, 1975, 41:4.

[128] *New York Times*, February 7, 1976, 14:7.

[129] *New York Times*, November 15, 1974, 25:4.

[130] *Essence*, March 1975, p. 116.

[131] U. S., Bureau of the Census, *1980 Census Report* (Washington: Government Printing Office, 1982).

[132] Lee Kravitz, "On Camera: Photography As Art," *Signature* (August 1984): 6.

[133] C. Gerald Fraser, "A Century of Black Photographers," *New York Times* March 2, 1984, Sec. 3, p. 3.

[134] Ibid.

[135] U. S., Bureau of the Census, *Occupational Outlook Handbook*, 1984-1985, pp. 166–7.

Selected Bibliography

Books

A.M.E. Book Concern. *Who's Who in Philadelphia*. Philadelphia: African Methodist Episcopal Book Company, 1912.

Aptheker, Herbert, ed. *A Documentary History of the Negro People in the United States: 1910–1932*. Secaucus, New Jersey: Citadel Press, 1973.

Bambara, Toni Cade, ed. *The Black Woman*. New York: New American Library, 1970.

Bontemps, Arna, and Fonville-Bontemps, Jacqueline. *Forever Free: Art by African-American Women: 1862–1980*. Exhibit Catalogue.

Boone, Irving. *A Survey of Progress of North Carolina. Negro Business and Professional Men and Women*, vol. 2. North Carolina: Irving Boone, 1946.

Boris, Joseph, ed. *Who's Who in Colored America, 1928–1929*. New York: Who's Who In Colored America Corporation, 1929.

Buck, Pearl S., and Robeson, Eslanda. *American Argument*. New York: John Day Company, 1949.

Carroll, Benaiah H. *Standard History of Houston in Texas*. Knoxville, Tennessee: H. W. Crew & Company, 1912.

Coar, Valencia Hollins. *A Century of Black Photographers: 1840–1960*. Providence, Rhode Island: Rhode Island School of Design, Museum of Art, 1983.

Crawford, Joe, ed. *The Black Photographers Annual*. Vol. 1–4. Brooklyn, New York: Another View, 1971–1977.

Dannett, Sylvia G. L., ed. *Profiles of Negro Womanhood*. 2 Volumes. Yonkers: Negro Heritage Library, 1964.

Danville, Illinois, City Directories: 1899, 1903, 1904, 1905, 1906.

Davis, Marianna, ed. *Contributions of Black Women to America, 1776–1977*. 2 Volumes. Columbia, South Carolina: Kenday Press, 1982.

Drake, St. Clair, and Cayton, Horace R. *Black Metropolis*. New York: Harcourt, Brace and Company, 1945.

Gernsheim, Helmut, and Gernsheim, Alison. *A Concise History of Photography*. London: Thames and Hudson, 1965.

Giddings, Paula. *When and Where I Enter . . . The Impact of Black Women on Race and Sex in America*. New York: William Morrow & Company, 1984.

Green, Jonathan. *American Photography: A Critical History 1945 to the Present*. New York: Harry N. Abrams, 1984.

Greene, Robert Ewell. *Black Defenders of America, 1775–1973*. Chicago: Johnson Publishing Company, 1974.

Hamm, J. R. *National Negro Business League Proceedings*. Boston, 1900.

————. *National Negro Business League Proceedings*. Boston, 1905.

Harlan, Louis R., and Smock, Raymond W. *The Booker T. Washington Papers*. Vol. 5, *1899–1900*. Chicago: University of Illinois Press, 1902.

———. *The Booker T. Washington Papers.* Vol. 6, *1901–1902.* Chicago: University of Illinois Press, 1904.

Harlem Business Register. *New York's Harlem Business Register.* New York: 1951.

Harris, I. C., ed. *The Colored Men's Professional and Business Directory of Chicago.* Chicago: I. C. Harris, 1886.

Haynes, George E. *The Negro at Work in New York City.* New York: AMS Press, 1968.

Henri, Florette. *Black Migration: Movement North, 1900–1920.* Garden City, New York: Anchor Press/Doubleday, 1976.

Hilyer, Andrew. *20th Century Union League Directory.* Washington, D.C.: Andrew Hilyer, 1901.

Houston City Directory, 1866.

Katz, William Loren. *The Atlanta University Publications 1,2,4,8,9,11,13,14,15,16,17,18.* New York: Arno Press and The New York Times, 1968.

Katz, William Loren, ed. *Negro Population in the United States 1790–1915.* New York: Arno Press and The New York Times, 1968.

Keene, Josephine Bond, ed. *Directory of Negro Business and Professional Women.* Philadelphia: Josephine Bond Keene, 1939.

Ladner, Joyce A. *Tomorrow's Tomorrow: The Black Woman.* Garden City, New York: Anchor Books, 1972.

Lerner, Gerda, ed. *Black Women in White America: A Documentary History.* New York: Vintage Books, 1973.

Loewenberg, Bert James, and Ruth Bogin, eds. *Black Women in Nineteenth-Century American Life: Their Words, Their Thoughts, Their Feelings.* University Park: Pennsylvania State University Press, 1976.

Low, W. Augustus, and Clift, Virgil A., eds. *Encyclopedia of Black America.* New York: McGraw-Hill, 1981.

Majors, M. A. *Noted Negro Women, Their Triumphs and Activities.* Chicago: Donohue and Henneberry, 1893.

Newhall, Beaumont. *The History of Photography: From 1830 to the Present Day.* New York: Museum of Modern Art, 1964.

Noble, Jeanne. *Beautiful, Also, Are the Souls of My Black Sisters: A History of the Black Woman in America.* Englewood Cliffs, New Jersey: Prentice-Hall, 1978.

Oak, Vishnu V. *The Negro Adventure in General Business.* Yellow Springs, Ohio: Antioch Press, 1949.

Pennsylvania Negro Business Directory. Harrisburg, 1910.

Ploski, Harry A., and Marr, Warren. *The Negro Almanac: A Reference Work on the Afro-American.* New York: Bellwether Publishing Company, 1976.

Pollard, Myrtle Evangeline. *Harlem As Is.* New York: City University of New York Thesis, 1936.

Quarles, Benjamin. *The Negro in the Making of America.* New York: Collier Books, 1969.

Rodgers-Rose, LaFrances, ed. *The Black Woman.* Beverly Hills: Sage Publications, 1980.

Rose, Arnold, ed. *Assuring Freedom to the Free.* Detroit: Wayne State University, 1964.

Rose, Frank Alexander and Kennedy, Louise Venable. *A Bibliography of Negro Migration.* New York: Columbia University Press, 1934.

Sage: A Scholarly Journal on Black Women 1 (Spring 1984) Special Issue on Black Women's Education.

Sandler, Martin V. *The Story of American Photography.* Boston: Little, Brown and Company, 1979.

Scott, Bell Patricia, and Murray, Saundra, eds. "A Special Issue on Black Women." *Psychology of Women Quarterly* 6 (Spring 1982).

Sims, Janet L. *The Progress of Afro-American Women: A Selected Bibliography and Resource Guide.* Westport, Connecticut: Greenwood Press, 1980.

Smythe, Mabel, ed. *The Black American Reference Book.* Englewood Cliffs, New Jersey: Prentice-Hall, 1976.

Sterling, Dorothy. *We Are Your Sisters: Black Women in the Nineteenth Century.* New York: W. W. Norton, 1984.

Stoot, William. *Documentary Expression and Thirties America.* New York: Oxford University Press, 1973.

Texas Centennial Committee. *The Negro in Texas History, An Historical and Pictorial Souvenir of Texas 1836–1936.* Dallas: Mason Brewer Mathis Publishing Company, 1935.

United States in World War II, Special Studies. Washington: Government Printing Office, 1954.

U. S., Bureau of the Census. *1850 Census Report*. Washington: Government Printing Office, 1853.

_____ . *1870 Census Report, Population*. Washington: Government Printing Office, 1872.

_____ . *1900 Census Report, Population*. Washington: Government Printing Office, 1902.

_____ . *1910 Census Report, Population*. Washington: Government Printing Office, 1913.

_____ . *Negroes in the United States*, Bulletin 129. Washington: Government Printing Office, 1915.

_____ . *Negroes in the United States 1920–1932*. Washington: Government Printing Office, 1935.

_____ . *Occupational Outlook Handbook*. Washington: Government Printing Office, 1984.

U. S., Department of Labor. *The Negro at Work During the World War and During Reconstruction*. Washington: Government Printing Office, 1921.

U. S., Detroit Bureau of Governmental Research, *The Negro in Detroit*. Prepared for the Mayor's Interracial Committee by Special Survey Staff. Washington: Government Printing Office, 1926.

U. S., Summary and Census of Business, Vol. 3, *Service Establishments*. Washington: Government Printing Office, 1939.

_____ . *1954 U.S. Census of Business*. Washington: Government Printing Office, 1958.

_____ . *1960 Characteristics of Population*. Washington: Government Printing Office, 1961.

U. S., Women's Bureau. *Changes in Women's Occupations 1940–1950*. Washington: Government Printing Office, 1954.

U. S., Women's Bureau. *Negro Women and their Jobs*. Washington: Government Printing Office, 1954.

U. S., Women's Bureau. *Women's Job Advances and Growth*. Pamphlet No. 232. Washington: Government Printing Office, 1949.

Wallace, Phyllis A. *Black Women in the Labor Force*. Cambridge, Massachusetts: The MIT Press, 1980.

Watkins, Sylvestre, ed. *Pocket Book of Negro Facts*. Chicago: Bookmark Press, 1946.

Works Progress Administration. *Writers Program, Houston (Texas): A History and Guide*. 1942.

Periodicals

Alexander, Sadie T. M. "Negro Women in our Economic Life." *Opportunity* (July 1930): 201–203.

Bisland, Margaret. "Women and Their Cameras." *Outing Magazine* (October 17, 1890): 36–43.

Davie L. Helen. "Women in Photography." *Camera Craft* (1902): 130–38.

Essence, March 1975.

Harper, Frances Ellen. "Coloured Women of America." *English Woman's Review* (January 15, 1878): 10–15.

"Have Camera Will Travel." *Ebony* (March 1969): 112–20.

Hayes, Elizabeth Ross. "Two Million Negro Women At Work." *Southern Workman* (February 22, 1922): 65–72.

Hines, Richard, Jr. "Women in Photography." *Photo Era* 17 (September, 1906): 141–49.

Holland, W. W. "Photography for Our Young People." *Colored American* (May 1902).

Kravitz, Lee. "On Camera: Photography As Art." *Signature* (August 1984): 6.

Moore, Clarence B. "Women Experts in Photography." *Cosmopolitan* (March 1893): 580–90.

Morris, Lewis. "Paris and the International Exposition." *Colored American* (November 1900): 291–95.

Morrison, Allan. "Women in the Arts." *Ebony* (August 1966): 90.

"Occupational Classes Among Negroes in Cities." *American Journal of Sociology* (March 1930): 718–38.

Washburne, Marion Foster. "A New Profession for Women." *Godey's Magazine* (February 1897), 134, no. 800: 123–28.

Williams, Fannie B. "The Colored Girl." *Voice of the Negro* (June 1905): 400–3.

"Women and Photography," *American Amateur Photographer* 2 (1899): 118–24, 144–52.

Newspapers

"Artists of the Bowery." *The New York Times*, April 12, 1885, p. 14.

"Black Women Emerge from History's Neglect." *The New York Times*, March 6, 1985.

"The Ethics and Etiquette of Photography." *The Independent*, July 7, 1907.

"5,000 Hired by WPA; Total is Now 25,000." *The New York Times*, September 4, 1935, p.6.

Fraser, C. Gerald. "A Century of Black Photographers." *The New York Times*, March 2, 1984, Sec. 3, p. 3.

"Houston's Lady Photographer." *The Houston Informer*, February 16, 1965.

"Houston's Leading Black Woman." *Houston Chronicle*, June 12, 1969.

Jenkins, Alexis. "Image of Success." *The Big Red*, March 16, 1980.

"Louise Martin: Giving It Her Best Shot." *The Houston Post*, February 12, 1984, p. 4G.

McKenzie, Marjorie. "In Fifty Years, Women Move Forward in Arts and Professions." *Pittsburgh Courier*, January 27, 1951.

"Mr. Battey Passes." *The Tuskegee Messenger*, March 12–26, 1927, p. 5.

"The Negro at Paris in 1900." *Kansas City Observer*, January 27, 1900, p. 1.

The Tuskegee Student, December 17, 1921.

"WACS End Picture Study." *The New York Times*, October 10, 1944, p. 17.

The Weekly Anglo-American, February 11, 1860.

"What an Outfit Will Cost." *The New York Times*, April 26, 1891, p. 14.

"Women Who Press the Button." *The New York Times*, October 1, 1893, p. 18.

Index